W9-AEE-774

Love

The following Oswald Chambers books are available from Discovery House Publishers:

Biblical Ethics

Biblical Psychology

Christian Disciplines

Complete Works of Oswald Chambers

Conformed to His Image
    / The Servant as His Lord

Faith: A Holy Walk

If You Will Ask

Love: A Holy Command

The Love of God

My Utmost for His Highest

Our Brilliant Heritage / If You Will Be Perfect
    / Disciples Indeed

Our Ultimate Refuge

Prayer: A Holy Occupation

So Send I You / Workmen of God

Studies in the Sermon on the Mount

Love  *A Holy Command*

Oswald Chambers

Compiled and Edited by
JULIE ACKERMAN LINK

Discovery House Publishers

Books, music, and videos that feed the soul with the Word of God

Box 3566 Grand Rapids, MI 49501

Love: A Holy Command
© 2008 by Oswald Chambers Publications Association
Limited. All rights reserved.

Discovery House Publishers is affiliated with RBC
Ministries, Grand Rapids, Michigan.

Discovery House books are distributed to the trade
exclusively by Barbour Publishing, Inc., Uhrichsville, Ohio.

All Scripture quotations are from the New King James
Version. Copyright © 1979, 1980, 1982 by Thomas
Nelson, Inc., Publishers.

Questions by Julie Ackerman Link

Library of Congress Cataloging-in-Publication Data

Chambers, Oswald, 1874-1917.
   Love: a holy command / Oswald Chambers ;
compiled and edited by Julie Ackerman Link.
       p. cm.
   Includes index.
   ISBN 978-1-57293-258-6
1. Love--Religious aspects--Christianity. I. Link, Julie
Ackerman. II. Title.
   BV4639.C418 2008
   241'.4--dc22

                          2007051612

Printed in the United States of America
08 09 10 11 12 13 14 15 / CHG / 10 9 8 7 6 5 4 3 2 1

Contents

Introduction

Tell me to exercise, eat well, and be nice, and I understand the commands. I know what to do. I might not always obey, but I know what is expected of me. But being told to *love* doing these things leaves me in a quandary. I eat vegetables because I know they're good for me, but I certainly can't say that I *love* eating them. I can't even say that I *prefer* them over chocolate.

Various definitions indicate that love is an intense feeling of affection or desire or a strong emotional attachment. According to Oswald Chambers, "Love is the sovereign preference of my person for another person, and Jesus Christ demands that that other person be Himself."[SSY]

When asked about the greatest commandment, Jesus summarized it with a single word: Love. He then stated the priorities of love—love God with all your heart, soul, mind, and strength, and love your neighbor as yourself. To comprehend love as a command requires a major shift in thinking. How can we obey a command to *feel* or *prefer* something? We tend to think of love as something that happens *to* us, not something that we can call up on command or dish out on demand. Love has an emotional component that we cannot create.

The reason genuine love is difficult is because it is in fact impossible. We cannot love apart from God because God *is* love. We love because He first loved us. We can behave in loving ways, but that is not the same as loving. After all, no one would argue that being nice is the same as being in love!

In *Workmen for God*, Chambers wrote:

> This work of feeding and tending sheep is hard, arduous work, and love for the sheep alone will not do it, you must have a consuming love for the great Shepherd, the Lord Jesus Christ . . . Love for men as men will never stand the strain . . .
> You must have a consuming passion of love, then He will flow through you in a passion of love and yearning and draw men to Himself.

Genuine love comes *from* God and flows *through* us. When we behave badly toward someone, it's not because we have failed in our efforts to love; it's because we have suppressed the love of God which He wants to express through us.

When we begin to comprehend God's great love for us, we in turn love Him. And our love for Him will change the world.

—Julie Ackerman Link

Love
with all your HEART

WHERE DO WE find ourselves with regard to this first great duty—"Thou shalt love the Lord thy God with all thy heart"? What does that phrase mean to us? If Jesus had said, "Thou shalt love thy lover with all thy heart," we would have known what He meant. Well, He did mean that, but the Lover is to be God. The majority of us have an ethereal, unpractical, bloodless abstraction which we call "love for God"; to Jesus love for God meant the most passionate intense love of which a human being is capable.CHI

Reflection Questions

How would I characterize my relationship with God? Polite or passionate? What makes me zealous? What would make me feel more zeal for God?

AN UNEMOTIONAL LOVE is inconceivable. Love for the good must involve displeasure and grief for the evil. God is not an almighty sultan reigning aloof, He is right in the throes of life, and it is there that emotion shows itself.OPG

Love with all your HEART

THE LOOK OF Jesus will mean a heart broken for ever from allegiance to any other person or thing. Has Jesus ever looked at you? The look of Jesus transforms and transfixes. Where you are "soft" with God is where the Lord has looked at you. If you are hard and vindictive, insistent on your own way, certain that the other person is more likely to be in the wrong than you are, it is an indication that there are whole tracts of your nature that have never been transformed by His gaze.^{CG}

Reflection Questions

Is my heart too hard to admit when I am wrong? Why is it so difficult for me to accept that I am not always right? What does this indicate about my ability to love?

LOYALTY TO JESUS CHRIST is the supernatural work of Redemption wrought in me by the Holy Ghost Who shed abroad the love of God in my heart, and that love works efficaciously through me in contact with everyone I meet.^{CG}

Love: A Holy Command

THE MARVELOUS, UNCRUSHABLE characteristic of a saint is that he does discern God. You may put a saint in tribulation, amid an onslaught of principalities and powers, in peril, pestilence or under the sword, you may put a saint anywhere you like, and he is "more than conqueror" every time. Why? Because his heart being filled with the love of God, he has the power to perceive and understand that behind all these things is God making them "work together for good."[BP]

Reflection Questions

What do I "hear" during times of trouble? Do I hear the assurance that even this can work for good? Or do I hear that it's time for me to take matters into my own hands?

MANY A MAN has awakened love before the time, and has reaped hell into the bargain. Love is awakened before the time whenever a man or woman ignores the worship of God and becomes a mere creature of impulsive passions.[OPG]

Love with all your HEART

LOVE FOR GOD does not spring naturally out of the human heart; but it is open to us to choose whether we will have the love of God imparted to us by the Holy Spirit. ". . . the love of God is shed abroad in our hearts by the Holy Ghost which is given unto us" (Romans 5:5; see also Luke 11:13). We are emphasizing just now the need of voluntary choice. It is of no use to pray, "O Lord, for more love! give me love like Thine; I do want to love Thee better," if we have not begun at the first place, and that is to choose to receive the Holy Spirit Who will shed abroad the love of God in our hearts.[BP]

Reflection Questions

Have I opened my heart to receive the love of God offered in and through Christ? Or am I still trying to manufacture love by devoting myself to a good cause?

THE HIGHEST CHRISTIAN love is not devotion to a work or to a cause, but to Jesus Christ.[PH]

WHAT A REST comes when the love of God has been shed abroad in my heart by the Holy Spirit! I realize that God is love, not loving, but love, something infinitely greater than loving, consequently He has to be very stern. There is no such thing as God overlooking sin. That is where people make a great mistake with regard to love; they say, "God is love and of course He will forgive sin": God is holy love and He *cannot* forgive sin. Jesus Christ did not come to forgive sin; He came to save us from our sins. The salvation of Jesus Christ removes the "sinner" out of my heart and plants in the "saint." That is the marvelous work of God's grace.[BP]

Reflection Questions

Do I impose my own concept of love on God?
Or do I define love by the character of God?

WE ARE TAUGHT that Jesus Christ was meek and loving, and He was; but we forget the times when He was ablaze with zeal for His Father's honor.[PH]

Love with all your HEART

IF WE HAVE really had wrought into our hearts and heads the amazing revelation which Jesus Christ gives that God is love and that we can never remember anything He will forget, then worry is impossible. Notice how frequently Jesus Christ warns against worry. The "cares of this world" will produce worry, and the "lusts of other things" entering in will choke the word God has put in. Is the thing which claims my attention just now the one thing for which God saved and sanctified me? If it is, life is all the time becoming simpler, and the crowding, clamoring lusts have no hold.[BP]

Reflection Questions

What causes me to worry? What drains my energy and consumes my time? Do I spend my time fulfilling God's purpose for my life or trying to fulfill some vague hidden expectations?

THERE IS NEVER any risk in love that is "talked." If love is reticent it becomes a secret treasure that enervates. Keep it in the open, have nothing hidden to brood over.[RTR]

IT IS PATHETIC the number of people who are piously trying to make their poor human hearts love God! The Holy Spirit sheds abroad in my heart, not the power to love God, but the very nature of God; A saint is not a human being who is trying to be good, trying by effort and prayer and longing and obedience to attain as many saintly characteristics as possible; a saint is a being who has been re-created. "If any man is in Christ, he is a new creation."[BP]

Reflection Questions

What unspoken fear or desire is keeping me from intimacy with God? What am I afraid God will ask of me? What am I afraid He will refuse to give to me?

OUR NOTION OF sacrifice is the wringing out of us something we don't want to give up, full of pain and agony and distress. The Bible idea of sacrifice is that I give as a love-gift the very best thing I have.[RTR]

WHEN THE HOLY SPIRIT comes in, unbelief is turned out and the energy of God is put into us, and we are enabled to will and to do of His good pleasure. When the Holy Spirit comes in He sheds abroad the love of God in our hearts, so that we are able to show our fellows the same love that God has shown to us. When the Holy Spirit comes in He makes us as "light," and our righteousness will exceed the righteousness of the most moral upright natural man because the supernatural has been made natural in us.[BP]

Reflection Questions

Is my life of faith more natural than supernatural? Do I have the kind of fear that keeps me a "safe" distance from God or curled up in the safety of His love?

"PERFECT LOVE CASTETH OUT FEAR," but to say "therefore will we not fear, though the earth be removed," is only possible when the love of God is having its way.[RTR]

THE SERVANTS OF God in the Bible never stole hearts to themselves, but handed them over to God. It is not *you* who awakened that mighty desire in the heart; it is not *you* who called forth that longing in that spirit; it is God in you. Are you a servant of God? If that longing, loving heart awakens and finds you instead of God, what a passion of despair will blight you with the curse of solitariness and silence!CD

Reflection Questions

Do I hide God in my heart? Or do I hide myself in God? Am I more interested in having people see Christ in me or of having them see God in Christ?

IT NEVER COST a disciple anything to follow Jesus; to talk about cost when you are in love with anyone is an insult. The point of suffering is that it costs other people—fathers, mothers, households; consequently we decline to go on, consideration for others causes us to hold back.SHL

Love with all your HEART

A SERVANT OF Jesus Christ is one who is willing to go to martyrdom for the reality of the Gospel of God. When a merely moral man or woman comes in contact with baseness and immorality and treachery, the recoil is so desperately offensive to human goodness that the heart shuts up in despair. The marvel of the Redemptive Reality of God is that the worst and the vilest can never get to the bottom of His love. Paul did not say that God separated him to show what a wonderful man He could make of him, but "to reveal His Son in me."CG

Reflection Questions
In what way is the love of God being revealed in me? Am I willing to have God's love perfected in me, no matter the cost?

THE LOVE OF God is the great mainspring, and by our voluntary choice we can have that love shed abroad in our hearts. Then, unless hindered by disobedience, it will go on to develop into the perfect love described in 1 Corinthians 13.BP

WE LIMIT OURSELVES and our conceptions of God by ignoring the side of the Divine Nature best symbolized by womanhood, and the Comforter, be it reverently said, surely represents this side of the Divine Nature. It is the Comforter Who sheds abroad the love of God in our hearts. It is the Comforter Who baptizes us into oneness with Jesus, in the amazing language of Scripture, until we are indwelt by a mysterious union with God. It is the Comforter Who brings forth the fruit of love, joy, peace, long-suffering, kindness, goodness, faithfulness, meekness, temperance.[CD]

Reflection Questions

How do misconceptions about God lead to minunderstandings among the children of God?

THE DEEP SECRET of God is Love, and only the child-heart and the child-spirit can find the way to learn this secret. Jesus Christ satisfies the last aching abyss of the human spirit, and until He does there is a great element of the precarious in our life.[CD]

Love with all your HEART

WHEN WE HAVE that wonderful love of God in our hearts, the sovereign preference for Jesus Christ, our love for others will be relative to this central love. "We preach not ourselves, but Christ Jesus the Lord; and ourselves your servants *for Jesus' sake*" (2 Corinthians 4:5).[BP]

Reflection Questions

Is my love for God rooted in Jesus? Is my love for others rooted in what Jesus can do for them or in what I can get from them? What do I expect from God that I am unwilling to give to others?

THE SUREST SIGN that God has done a work of grace in my heart is that I love Jesus Christ best, not weakly and faintly, not intellectually, but passionately, personally and devotedly, overwhelming every other love of my life.[BP]

THE BIBLE KNOWS only one love, and that is the supreme, dominating love of God. Jesus Christ teaches that if we have had a work of grace done in our hearts, we will show to our fellow-men the same love God has shown to us. "A new commandment I give unto you, that ye love one another; as I have loved you, that ye also love one another" (John 13:34).[BP]

Reflection Questions

How does my love for others fall short of God's love for me? How would my life change if my love for God were to dominate all my decisions and interactions?

LOVE FOR THE Lord is not an ethereal, intellectual, dream-like thing; it is the the most intense, the most vital, the most passionate love of which the human heart is capable. The realization of such a fathomless love is rarely conscious, saving in some supreme crisis akin to martyrdom.[BP]

WHAT IS THE difference between liberty and license? Liberty is the ability to perform the law, perfect freedom to fulfill all the demands of the law. To be free from the law means that I am the living law of God, there is no independence of God in my make-up. License is rebellion against all law. If my heart does not become the center of Divine love, it may become the center of diabolical license.[BP]

Reflection Questions

Do I consider God's love and sympathy a license to sin or a liberating power that loosens the bonds of sin and failure so I can accomplish good? How does God's sympathy toward my weakness guide me into goodness?

FROM GUIDANCE BY His sympathy, we learn that God heeds not our faults nor our mistakes, He looks at our hearts. This point, so blessed, so rare, perhaps we could never see before. How gladly, how nobly, how purely we grow under the guidance by God's sympathy![CD]

I AM CREATED for God; He made me. This realization of the election of God is the most joyful realization on earth, and we have to learn to rely on the tremendous creative purpose of God. The first thing God will do with us is to "force thro' the channels of a single heart" the interests of the whole world. The love of God, the very nature of God, is introduced into us, and the nature of Almighty God is that *"God so loved the world."*^{CG}

Reflection Questions

Am I imprisoned by some false idea of truth or set free by the reality of God's love for the world and His desire for peace? Do I use God's love as a means to make peace? Or do I misuse God's love as an excuse to wage war?

GOD'S GREAT WORK is the production of saints. It is humbling beyond words to be told by our Father that it was not for love of the Truth that we had been bold, but that the great labor allowed us was the means of releasing our imprisoned hearts and was for our own peace.^{CD}

JESUS CHRIST AND He alone is able to satisfy the craving of the human heart to know the meaning of life. He enables men to understand that they have come into this life from a deep purpose in the heart of God; that the one thing they are here for is to get readjusted to God and become His lovers.[CHI]

Reflection Questions

What desires of my heart need to be readjusted so I can become a passionate lover of God? What sin may be keeping me from realizing the full measure of God's love?

GOD'S LOVE SEEMS so strange to our natural conceptions that it has to be commended to us before we see anything in it. It is only when we have been awakened by conviction to the sin and anarchy of our hearts against God that we realize the measure of His love toward us.[OBH]

PROFESSIONS LAST AS long as the conditions that called them forth last, but no longer. As long as the fervid, strong attachment to Jesus lasts, the professions are the natural expression of that attachment; but when the way grows narrow, and reputations are torn, and the popular verdict is against the shameful poverty and meekness of the Son of Man, professions wither on the tongue; not through cowardice, but because the conditions that made the heart warm, and the feelings move and the mouth speak, are altered. When the way of joyfully leaving all and following Jesus in the bounding days of devotion turns into the way of sorrow, then the heart's feelings are frozen or changed into horror and perplexity. Love never professes; love *confesses*.^{CD}

Reflection Questions

In what ways does my love for God depend on circumstance? How is my love for God affected when my circumstances change?

FAITH FEARS NOTHING because the heart is blazing with the love of God.^{CD}

HOW WE MISS IT! Those loyal true, human hearts, and ourselves, until we are changed by the deep upheaval of a birth from above, and the presence of an over-whelming love to our Lord in our hearts. The desire to be the "loyalest," the "faithfullest," the "holiest" disciple produces a winsome rebuke from our Lord, and our hearts feel we have missed the point but scarcely know how. It was surely natural for the disciples to imagine "who should be the greatest"; and yet when Jesus questioned them, their hearts confused and rebuked them.[CD]

Reflection Questions

In what ways am I still trying to earn God's love by being the first or best? What will it take for me to be willing to be last or least?

GOD GRANT WE may not only experience the indwell-ing of the love of God in our hearts, but go on to a hearty abandon to that love so that God can pour it out through us for His redemptive purposes for the world. He broke the life of His own Son to redeem us, and now He wants to use our lives as a sacrament to nourish others.[CHI]

To MAKE DISCIPLES, we must have been made disciples ourselves. There is no royal road to sainthood and discipleship. The way of the Cross is the only way. We see God only from a pure heart, never from an able intellect. In wonder, love and awe we thank God for "the glory and the passion of this midnight," because we are brought to the threshold of an understanding of the loneliness of Jesus Christ Who was "made to be sin on our behalf; that we might become the righteousness of God in Him."CD

Reflection Questions

Is my view of God distorted because the desires of my heart are corrupted? Am I willing to accept loneliness as part of the necessary purging process? Will it lead me to repentance or rebellion?

How MANY OF us have allowed the goodness of God to lead us to repentance? Or are we so enjoying the blessings of God, taking them as our due and not seeing behind them the great loving hand of God, whose heart is overflowing in tremendous love?GW

Love with all your HEART

LOVINGKINDNESS IS THE purest, rarest evidence of the indwelling of the Spirit of God—no more neutrality, no more dread of the nemesis, just the Divine nature, beautiful, pleasant beneficence, all summed up in the word "Love." When the love of God is shed abroad in our hearts it means that we identify ourselves with God's interest in other people, and God is interested in some strange people!HGM

Reflection Questions

Am I having trouble seeing God because I'm focused on people? What would change if I saw other people through the eyes of God rather than looking for God in the eyes of other people?

WHEN A MAN is born from above there is no sadness in natural love; it ends nowhere but in the heart of God; "in Christ" life knows no death, it goes on more and more fully. If you want to know God's original design for man, you see it in Jesus Christ.HGM

JESUS CHRIST NEVER expected from human nature what it was not designed to give; consequently He was never bitter or cynical. Unless our human relationships are based in God they will end in frantic disillusionment. The cause of it is the demand in human nature for satisfaction. No human being can ever give satisfaction, and when I demand it and do not get it I become cruel and spiteful.[HGM]

Reflection Questions

How would my relationships with family and friends change if my love for God were perfected? In what ways am I cruel and spiteful to those whose love is imperfect?

WHEN WE ARE rightly related to Jesus Christ, human love is transfigured because the last aching abyss of the heart is satisfied; but if the relationship with God is cut out our relationship to others is embittered. When once the relationship with God is right the satisfaction of human love is marvelous.[HGM]

THE LOVE OF a mother is her own peculiar love, and the love of a father is his own peculiar love. Every different kind of love illustrates some aspect of God's love; but it must not be forgotten that the love of God is His own peculiar love. Because of the disposition arising from anarchy against God, men do not see or believe that the Cross of Christ is the expression of God's own love; but when a man is convicted of sin, he begins to discern the marvelously patient love of God.ᶜᴰ

Reflection Questions

Am I as eager for God to be patient with others as I am for Him to be patient with me? In what ways do I allow earthly passions to guide my decisions?

TO LOVE GOD with all my heart means to be weaned from the dominance of earthly things as a guide; there is only one dominant passion in the deepest center of the personality, and that is the love of God.ᴵᵀᵂᴮᴾ

LOVE REQUIRES CAREFUL developing; love won't stay if it is not sedulously cultivated. If I am not careful to keep the atmosphere of my love right by cultivation, it will turn to lust—"I must have this thing for myself." No love of the natural heart is safe unless the human heart has been satisfied by God first. Jesus Christ alone can satisfy the aching abyss of the human heart.ᴴᴳᴹ

Reflection Questions

*What "love" do I have that is not from God?
What am I trying to get from someone that
only God can give? When I hate the wrong
in someone else, what sacrifice am I willing to
make to see the wrong made right?*

GOD SO LOVES the world that He hates the wrong in it. Do I so love men and women that I hate the wrong in them? Most of us love other people for what they are to us instead of for what God wants them to be. The distress worked in a man's heart by the Holy Ghost is never on his own account, but always on God's account.ᶜᴴᴵ

EMOTION IS NOT simply an overplus of feeling; it is life lived at a white-heat state of wonder. To lose wonder is to lose the true element of religion. Has the sense of wonder been dying down in your religious life? If so, you need to get back to the Source. If you have lost the fervor of delight in God, tell Him so. The old Divines used to ask God for the grace of trembling, that is, the sense of wonder. When wonder goes out of natural love, something or someone is to be blamed; wonder ought never to go.ᴴᴳ

Reflection Questions

What temptations have weakened me and caused me to lose my wonder? What doubts are clouding God's glory?

IN ALL THE temptations that contend in our hearts, and amidst the things that meet us in the providence of God which seem to involve a contradiction of His Fatherhood, the secret place convinces us that He is our Father and that He is righteousness and love, and we remain not only unshaken but we receive our reward with an intimacy that is unspeakable and full of glory.ᶜᴰ

WHEN ONCE GOD'S mighty grace gets my heart wholly absorbed in Him, every other love of my life is safe; but if my love to God is not dominant, my love may prove to be lust. Nearly all the cruelty in the world springs from misunderstanding this. Lust simply means I seek for a creature to give me what God alone can give, and I become cruel and vindictive and jealous and spiteful to the one from whom I demand what God alone can give.ITWBP

Reflection Questions

From whom do I expect what only God can give? How is this unfair expectation hurtful? What will make me be less demanding of love from others and more willing to give love to those in need?

TO REALIZE THAT it is possible for everyone to be in the light and experiencing the love of God, keeps us close to God's heart in intercession for those who will not heed.NJ

THE NOBILITY OF moral integrity and sterling natural virtue was lovely in the sight of Jesus because He saw in it a remnant of His Father's handiwork. How long are some of us, who ought to be princes and princesses for God, going to be bound up in the show of things instead of rising in the might of the Holy Ghost, with our feet on the earth but our hearts swelling with the love of heaven?ITWBP

Reflection Questions

What earthly burdens keep me from singing of God's heavenly love? What does my singing say to God about my view of the world? What does it say to the world about my view of God?

THE WORLD DOES not bid you sing, but God does. Song is the sign of an unburdened heart; then sing your songs of love unbidden, ever rising higher and higher into a fuller conception of the greatest, grandest fact on the stage of Time—God is Love.LG

THE LOVE OF God gives us a new method of seeing Nature. His voice is on the rolling air, we see Him in the rising sun, and in the setting He is fair; in the singing of the birds, in the love of human hearts, the voice of God is in all. Had we but ears to hear the stars singing, to catch the glorious pealing anthem of praise echoing from the hills of immortality by the heavenly hosts![LG]

Reflection Questions

How does God's love change my view of the world—of myself, others, and inexplicable circumstances? How does God's view of the world change my attitude toward others?

GOD DID NOT create man as a puppet to please a despotic idea of His own. He created us out of the superabundant flow of overflowing love and goodness. He created us susceptible of all the blessedness which He had ordained for us. He "thought" us in the rapture of His own great heart, and lo, we are![LG]

THE LOVE OF God performs a miracle of grace in graceless human hearts. Human love and lesser loves must wither into the most glorious and highest love of all—the love of God. Then we shall see not only each other's faults, we shall see the highest possibilities in each other, and shall love each other for what God will yet make of us.[LG]

Reflection Questions

Do I see myself in the light of God's love? Or do I see God through the cloud of my sinfulness? Am I eager to swim in the refreshing oceans of love or content to stand on the beach and get only my feet wet?

WHEN ONCE YOU have understood the truth about your own heart's sinfulness, think not again of it, but look at the great, vast, unlimited magnificence of the love of God. Oh may we be driven, driven further and further out into the ocean fullness of the love of God! only taking care that nothing entices us out again.[LG]

WHEN WE COME into contact with objectionable people the first natural impulse of the heart is to ask God to
save them because they are a trial to us; He will never
do it for that reason. But when we come to see those
lives from Jesus Christ's standpoint and realize that He
loves them as He loves us, we have a different relationship to them, and God can have His way in their lives in
answer to our prayer.^{MFL}

Reflection Questions
Do I see others in the light of God's love?
Or do I see God under the shadow of unloving
people? Do I want others thrown into a
dungeon of darkness or brought into
the light of God's love?

IF THE ANTAGONISM of the heart of man to the holiness of God is not removed, man's imagination will not
only picture God wrongly but he will come to know the
wrath of God instead of the love of God.^{NE}

THE NATURE OF God is exhibited in the life of Our Lord, and the great characteristic of His life is obedience. When the love of God is shed abroad in my heart by the Holy Ghost (Romans 5:5), I am possessed by the nature of God, and I know by my obedience that I love Him. The best measure of a spiritual life is not its ecstasies, but its obedience.[NKW]

Reflection Questions

Why is obedience the best measure of my love for God? When I disobey, what message am I sending to God? When obedience is an effort, what message should I be hearing about myself?

THE SPRINGS OF love are in God, not in us. It is absurd to look for the love of God in our natural hearts.[OBH]

LOOK BACK OVER your own history as revealed to you by grace, and you will see one central fact growing large—God is love. No matter how often your faith in such an announcement was clouded, no matter how the pain and suffering of the moment made you speak in a wrong mood, still this statement has borne its own evidence along with it most persistently—God is love. In the future, when trial and difficulties await you, do not be fearful, whatever and whoever you may lose faith in, let not this faith slip from you—God is Love; whisper it not only to your heart in its hour of darkness, but live in the belief of it.[LG]

Reflection Questions

When has suffering caused me to doubt God's love? When has God used trials to prove His love? What snap judgments have led to wrong conclusions?

THERE ARE TIMES when the Heavenly Father will look as if He were an unjust Judge, but He is not. In the meantime there is a cloud on the friendship of the heart, and even love itself has to wait often in pain and tears for the blessing of fuller communion.[PH]

IF THE GRACE and majesty and life and power and energy of God are not being manifested in us to the glory of God, we are wrong somewhere. If we want something conscious from God, it means the will has not been surrendered; immediately we do surrender, the tidal wave of the love of God carries us straight into all the fullness of God.OBH

Reflection Questions

Am I being swept by the tidal wave of God's love into the fullness of His majestic power? Or am I hanging on to some early experience that I have mistaken for the full expression of God's glory?

JESUS CHRIST MUST always be greater than our experience of Him, but our experience will be along the line of the faith we have in Him.OBH

THE LOVE OF God in us will produce an amazing sweetness in disposition towards Jesus Christ; but if we try to put that sweetness into the "bottle" we give to some earthly friend, the bottle will break and the wine will be lost. Is the love that is being exhibited by us the love of God or the love of our own natural hearts? God does not give us power to love as He loves; the love of God, the very nature of God, possesses us, and He loves through us.OBH

Reflection Questions

How have my efforts to love failed? Was I expressing the love of God or the love of my own needy self? Am I trying to possess God or am I pouring out all my worldly possessions so that God can possess all of me?

MARY DID NOT know that she was anointing the body of Jesus for His burial. Her heart was bursting with love to Jesus, and she took this opportunity of giving it expression.PH

Love with all your HEART

IT IS ABSURD to try and find the love of God in our hearts; it is not there any more than the life of Jesus Christ is there. Love and life are in God and in Jesus Christ and in the Holy Spirit whom God gives us, not because we merit Him, but according to His own particular graciousness.^{RTR}

Reflection Questions

Am I more attracted to those who love me or those who love God? Who will make a better friend? Are people attracted to me because I am likeable or because they see the likeness of Christ in me?

GOD CANNOT GUARD the natural heart that does not worship Him; it is at the mercy of every vagrant passion stirred by the nearness of another. Watch your fancies and your friends, heed who you love and who loves you, and you will be saved from many a pitfall.^{OPG}

GOD'S LOVE IS wrath towards wrong; He is never tender to that which hates goodness. When communion with God is severed the basis of life is chaos and wrath. The chaotic elements may not show at once, but they will presently. When we speak of the wrath of God we must not picture Him as an angry sultan on the throne of heaven, bringing a lash about people when they do what He does not want. There is no element of personal vindictiveness in God. It is rather that God's constitution of things is such that when a man is severed from God his life tumbles into turmoil and confusion, into agony and distress. It is hell at once, and he will never get out of it unless he turns to God. When he turns, chaos is turned into cosmos, wrath into love, distress into peace.[CHI]

Reflection Questions
Does my love for God include hatred for sin?
Do I hate my own sin as much as I hate
the sin of others?

TO DELIGHT IN sacrificing the natural to the spiritual means to be overflowing with the grace and love of God.[ITWBP]

Love with all your HEART

PEOPLE HAVE THE idea that Christianity and Stoicism are alike, but just at the point where they seem most alike, they are most divergent. A stoic overcomes the world by making himself indifferent, by passionlessness; the saint overcomes the world by the passion of his love for Jesus Christ.HG

Reflection Questions

In what situations have I chosen stoicism over passion? In what ways does stoicism seem safer? What frightens me about passion?

WHEN YOU REALIZE that God has forgiven your sins, given you the Holy Spirit, I defy you not to be carried away with emotion. Religion which makes for logic and reason is not religion, but to try to make religion out of emotion is to take a false step. Our Lord bases everything on life as it is, and life is implicit. For instance, you cannot explicitly state what love is, but love is the implicit thing that makes life worth living. You cannot explicitly state what sin is, but sin is the implicit thing that curses life.HG

THE JOY OF Jesus is a miracle, it is not the outcome of my doing things or of my being good, but of my receiving the very nature of God. In every phase of human experience apart from Jesus, something hinders our getting full joy. We may have the fulfilment of our ambitions, we may have love and money, yet there is the sense of something unfulfilled, something not finished, not right. A man is only joyful when he fulfils the design of God's creation of him, and that is a joy that can never be quenched.[HGM]

Reflection Questions

Have I been burned by passion for something other than God? Have I been burned by people who made passion their religion? Am I willing to burn with passion to illuminate the world with God's love?

WE LOVE THE lovely because it is flattering to us to do so. God loves the unlovely, and it broke His heart to do it. The depth of the love of God is revealed by that wonderful word, "whosoever." The Bible reveals God to be the Lover of His enemies.[HG]

LET OUR LORD be allowed to give the Holy Spirit to a man, deliver him from sin, and put His own love within him, and that man will love Him personally, passionately and devotedly. It is not an earning or a working for, but a gift and a receiving.[CHI]

Reflection Questions

Where have I gotten my definition of love? Why would I expect to find one outside the heart of God? Why would I rely on one that was written by anyone but the One whose very nature is love?

WE EMPHASIZE PERFECT love towards our fellow-men; the Bible emphasizes perfect love to God. Love is an indefinable word, and in the Bible it is always used as directly characteristic of God—"God is love."[ITWBP]

47

THE FUNDAMENTAL REVELATION made in the New Testament is that God redeemed the human race when we were spitting in His face. We can all be stirred by high, noble, human sacrifice; it is much more thrilling than Calvary. Calvary is an ignoble thing, against all the ideas of human virtue and nobility. God's love is not in accordance with our human standards in any way.[HGM]

Reflection Questions

What noble, human actions stir my emotions? How might my own actions change if my emotions were stirred by God's sacrificial love at work in and through me?

IT IS QUITE conceivable that many persons have such a slight regard for their fathers and mothers that it is nothing to them to separate from them; but the word "hate" shows by contrast the kind of love we ought to have for our parents, an intense love; yet, says Jesus, our love for Him is to be so intense that every other relationship is "hatred" in comparison if it should conflict with His claims.[BP]

WE MAKE THE mistake of imagining that service for others springs from love of others; the fundamental fact is that supreme love for our Lord alone gives us the motive power of service to any extent for others.[CHI]

Reflection Questions

What is my strongest motivation for doing good? Is it because I want to earn God's love for me or is it because I want to express God's love to others? How might my failure to "overcome" the world be related to my attempts to apply my own faulty concept of love to situations that desperately need the faultless love of God?

PASSIONS ARE TO be regulated by this first duty of love for God. The way we are to overcome the world, the flesh and the devil is by the force of our love for God regulating all our passions until every force of body, soul and spirit is devoted to this first great duty.[CHI]

THE SNEER OF Satan was that no man loved God for His own sake, but only for what God gave him. Satan was allowed to destroy all Job's blessings and yet Job did not curse God; he clung to it that the great desire of his heart was God Himself and not His blessings. Job lost everything he possessed, including his creed; the one thing he did not lose was his hold on God."SHH

Reflection Questions

Do I desire God more than God's blessings? Am I able to find joy even in loss? Do I trust that God will hold onto me when I have nothing to hold onto?

LORD, TODAY LET Thy praise abound, let joy and gladness here resound. How I long for joy—great bounding liberating joy: joy in God, joy in the Holy Ghost, joy in life, and joy in love.KGD

Love
with all your SOUL

"YOU ARE MY child, the friend of My Son, now exhibit to that mean and selfish person exactly the love I showed you when you were mean and selfish." We shall find ample room to eat "humble pie" all the days of our life. The thing that keeps us going is to recognize the humor of our heavenly Father. When we meet the disagreeable person we know what God is doing, He is giving us a mirror that we may see what we have been like toward Him.ᴼᴮᴴ

Reflection Questions

What difficult person in my life is reflecting to me an image of myself I'd rather not see?

THE TRUE IMPORT of love is the surrender of my self. I go out of myself in order to live in and for God. To be indwelt by the Spirit of Jesus means I am willing to quit my own abode and live only in and for God. It is not the surrender to a conqueror, but the surrender of love, a sovereign preference for God. I surrender myself—not because it is bad, self is the best thing I have got, and I give it to God; then self-realization is lost in God-realization.ᴳᵂ

Love with all your SOUL

WHEN ADAM'S SPIRIT, soul and body were united in perfect faith and love to God, his soul was the medium through which the marvelous life of the Spirit of God was brought down. The very image of God was brought down into his material body and it was clothed in an inconceivable splendor of light until the whole man was in the likeness of God.[BP]

Reflection Questions

In what ways is God's likeness being made visible in me? In what ways is God's love being expressed through me? What is the difference between the way I love and the way God loves? How would I describe "the center" of my life? How might others describe what they see as "the center" of my life?

THE CENTER OF my self should be God and love for Him.[BP]

How could the Pharisee in our Lord's parable possibly love his neighbor as himself? It was impossible, he had not found the true center for himself. His center was self-realization, and instead of loving the publican he increased his own conceit in every detail of comparison. Immediately I become rightly related to God and have perfect love toward Him, I can have the same relationship to my fellow-men that God has to me, and can love my fellow-men as I love myself.[BP]

Reflection Questions

Who do I love most? God, myself, or others? What would be a better order? Am I more interested in those who meet my spiritual needs or in those whose spiritual needs God would have me meet?

Our Lord has told us how love to Him is to manifest itself. "Lovest thou Me? . . . Feed My sheep"—identify yourself with My interests in other people, not, identify *Me* with *your* interests in other people. The character of this love is the love *of God* expressing itself.[CG]

ATONEMENT TAKES AWAY fearfulness and unbelief, and brings us back again into the relationship of faith and love to God. The new birth will bring us to the place where spirit, soul and body are identified with Christ, sanctified here and now and preserved in that condition, not by intuitions now, not by sudden impulses and marvelous workings of the new life within, but by a conscious, superior, moral integrity, transfigured through and through by our union with God through the Atonement.[BP]

Reflection Questions

Have I made the voluntary choice to receive the love of God? Have I come to the end of myself? Am I really a spiritual pauper? Do I realize that I have no power at all in myself to be holy? Do I deliberately choose to receive from God the sovereign grace that will work these things in me?[BP]

WHEN THE LOVE of God is in me I must learn how to let it express itself; I must educate myself in the matter; it takes time.[PH]

THE REVELATIONS MADE by Jesus Christ reveal that the right center for self is God—personal, passionate devotion to Him; then I am able to show to my fellow-men the same love that God has shown to me. Until I get there, I take the position of the Pharisee or of the publican; I either thank God that I am not an out-and-out sinner and point out certain people who are worse than I am, or else I grovel to the other extreme. Both attitudes are wrong because they are not truly centered.[BP]

Reflection Questions

In what ways is my self-image distorted? Do I think too highly or too lowly of myself? Or do I suffer from both at different times and in different situations? What attitude adjustment do I need so that I can love rightly?

IF THE MAINSPRING of your service is love for God, no ingratitude, no sin, no devil, no angel, can hinder you from serving your fellow-men, no matter how they treat you. You can love your neighbor as yourself, not from pity, but from the true centering of yourself in God.[BP]

PERFECT LOVE TAKES no account of the evil done unto it. It was the reproaches that hit and scandalized the true center of His life that Jesus Christ noticed in pain. What was that true center? Absolute devotion to God the Father and to His will; and as surely as you get Christ-centered you will understand what the Apostle Paul meant when he talks about filling up "that which is lacking of the afflictions of Christ." Jesus Christ could not be touched on the line of self-pity. The practical emphasis here is that our service is not to be that of pity, but of personal, passionate love to God, and a longing to see many more brought to the center where God has brought us.[BP]

Reflection Questions

What causes me to feel sorry for myself?
What shift in attitude do I need?

IF MY LOVE is first of all for God, I shall take no account of the base ingratitude of others, because the mainspring of my service to my fellow-men is love to God.[BP]

ALL THE TEACHING of Jesus weaves round the question of self. It is not "Oh, to be nothing, nothing!" but "Oh, to be something, something!" Aggressively and powerfully something, uncrushably something, something that stands next to God's throne, on the Rock; to be those in whom God can walk and talk and move and do what He likes, because self is personally, passionately in love with God, not absorbed into God; but centered in God.[BP]

Reflection Questions

Is my concern for others really love or just pity? How often am I kind to others just so I can feel better about myself?

UNLESS MY RELATIONSHIP to God is right, my sympathy for men will lead me astray and them also; but when once I am right with God, I can love my neighbor as God has loved me. How has God loved me? God has loved me to the end of all my sinfulness, the end of all my self-will, all my selfishness, all my stiff-neckedness, all my pride, all my self-interest; now He says I am to show to my fellow-men the same love.[BP]

GOD GETS ME into a relationship with Himself whereby I understand His call, then I do things out of sheer love for Him on my own account. To serve God is the deliberate love-gift of a nature that has heard the call of God. Service is expressive of that which is fitted to my nature: God's call is expressive of His nature; consequently when I receive His nature and hear His call, the voice of the Divine nature sounds in both and the two work together. The Son of God reveals Himself in me, and I serve Him in the ordinary ways of life out of devotion to Him.CG

Reflection Questions

In what unique way am I equipped to serve God? How much energy do I waste trying to be like someone else?

THE INCARNATION WAS not for the Self-realization of God, but for the purpose of removing sin and reinstating humanity into communion with God. Jesus Christ became Incarnate for one purpose, to make a way back to God that man might stand before Him as he was created to do, the friend and lover of God Himself.BSG

IT IS IN the mystic tenderness of the guidance by His sympathy that God gives a love like His own. Oh, how can language put it—when the soul, the individual soul, knows God has marked all sorrows and has kept all tears till not one drop is lost. When the first great surprise of the light of His sympathy bursts on our tear-dimmed soul and turns it into radiant rainbows of promise, and lo! a mystic touch is on our spirits, a coolness and balm, we know the tenderest touch of a mother's love is nothing compared to our blessed Father's sympathy!CD

Reflection Questions

Do I envy those whose walk with God is different from my own or am I secure in my unique relationship with the Lord?

GOD CREATED ME to be distinctly not Himself, but to realize Him in perfect love. If I allow that God teaches me to walk in His will, I shall allow my neighbor, whom I love as myself, the same certainty, although his way may seem so different.CD

Love with all your SOUL

WE HAVE THE idea nowadays that God is so loving and gentle and kind that all we need do is to say we feel sorry for the wrong we have done and we will try to be better. That is not repentance. The essence of repentance is that it destroys the lust of self-vindication; wherever that lust resides the repentance is not true. Repentance brings us to the place where we are willing to receive any punishment under heaven so long as the law we have broken is justified. Repentance involves the receiving of a totally new disposition so that I never do the wrong thing again.[CHI]

Reflection Questions

Do I repent because I have true sorrow and regret for degrading the image of God in me or because I feel bad that my own image has been marred?

IT IS PERILOUSLY possible to take the language of love and degrade it into a language that grovels; and it is perilously possible to take the language of the soul alone in these walks of eternal pleasure and degrade it into a wallowing horror.[CD]

WHENEVER YOU DEAL with a principle always take the best possible incarnation of it, never deal with it in the abstract. If I deify an abstraction called "love to God" I can jargon to further orders as though I really loved my fellowmen, but the crucial test when it comes will prove I don't. When I disassociate myself from God I become a law unto myself, and the first thing that happens is I don't love my neighbor as myself—I am so sure I am right and everyone else is wrong.ᴳᵂ

Reflection Questions

Am I more interested in having God make me attractive to others or make others attracted to Him?

THE LOVE OF self that Jesus not only justified but distinctly enjoined, is the direct product of the indwelling Holy Spirit; its perversion is the deification of my self. How is it possible for me to love my neighbor as myself? The best example of a lover of men is Jesus Christ, and the mainspring of His love for men was His love for God.ᴳᵂ

Love with all your SOUL

WHEN I LOVE Him supremely so that all other loves are hatred in comparison, then He can trust me with the hundredfold more because the interest of self-love no longer rules. Every human relationship is put by Jesus on an eternal basis, otherwise the relationships born from the center of what we call natural love end with this life, there is nothing more to them; but when they are rooted in the nature of God they are as eternal as God Himself.ᴳᵂ

Reflection Questions

What part of me is untrustworthy because my motives are impure? What part of my love is impure because it demands something in return?

FUNDAMENTALLY IT IS impossible to *love* a human being wrongly—nor is it possible to love a human being *rightly* if I love from the center of self-interest. The love which springs from self-interest ends in being cruel because it demands an infinite satisfaction from another human being which it will never get. The love which has God as its center makes no demands.ᴳᵂ

GOD WANTS US to dedicate ourselves to Him with quiet calm intelligence, with the deep fervent passion of knowing what we are doing. Have we the self-dedication of that moral passion? There are a great many passions that are not moral, enthusiasms that never sprang from God. We have to hold our emotions in check and let the Spirit of God bring us into one master-worship. The one love in the Bible is that of the Father and the Son; the one passion in the Bible is the passion of Jesus to bring men into the relationship of sons to the Father, and the one great passion of the saint is that the life of the Lord Jesus might be manifested in his mortal flesh.GW

Reflection Questions

In what ways does my life indicate that I long to see myself and others rightly related to God?

GOD NEVER REVEALS Himself in the same way to everyone, and yet the testimony of each one who has had a revelation of God is the same—that God is love.GW

Love with all your SOUL

OUR FAITH GETS contradicted by what we experience because we can know nothing except by God revealing Himself to us. We are in danger of taking each stage of our development in spiritual growth as final, and when a fuller flood as from God's own great life comes, overwhelming all the old traditional belief, we close down our soul over the earlier revelations—"I have the truth now." Consequently we stagnate because we cut ourselves off from God. There is no limit to what God can make us if we are willing. His great love is ever overshadowing us and He waits to visit us with His saving life.ᴳᵂ

Reflection Questions

In what ways do my old ideas about God keep me from learning anything new?

THE WHOLE OUTCOME of following Jesus is expressed in the words that the Trinity—Father, Son, and Holy Ghost—will come and make Their abode with the man who loves Jesus and keeps His word. As long as the devil can keep us terrified of thinking, he will always limit the work of God in our souls.ᴵᵀᵂᴮᴾ

IF GOD MAKES no difference in His external blessings to men, who are we that we should? One of the chief stagnating influences on spiritual character is this reasoning—"Do they deserve it?" How much do any of us deserve the blessings of God? Let us ever remember that to enter into the experience of God's beatitudes is to find ourselves able to show to our fellow-men the same unmerited mercy, the same unselfish, unmerited love that God has shown to us.ᴳᵂ

Reflection Questions

In what ways do I require people to earn my love and favor? Why am I unwilling to give it freely? What do I hope to gain by being stingy with love?

THE ONE CHARACTERISTIC of love is that it thinks of nothing for itself, it is absorbed in God.ᴵᵀᵂᴮᴾ

TAKE AN ABSOLUTE plunge into the love of God, and when you are there you will be amazed at your foolishness for not getting there before. It is not the question of the surrender of a soul for sanctification, but the unreserved surrender of a sanctified soul to God. We are so reserved where we ought to be unreserved, and so unreserved where we ought to be reserved. We ought never to be reserved towards God but utterly open, perfectly one with Him all through.[ITWBP]

Reflection Questions

What part of myself has not yet been sacrificed for Christ? What part have I reserved for myself?

THE ONLY WAY to love God with all our soul is to give up our lives for His sake, not give our lives to God, that is an elemental point, but when that has been done, after our lives have been given to God, we ought to lay them down for God. Every morning we wake, and every moment of the day, we have this glorious privilege of sacrificing our holy selves to and for Jesus Christ.[ITWBP]

WHEN THE SUPREME love of God in the giving of Himself has got hold of me, I love myself in the power of His love; that means a son of God being presented to God as a result of His effectual Redemption. That is a gratification to God because it is the returning back to Himself of His love in expressed reality. When the Redemption is effective in me, I am a delight to God, not to myself. I am not meant for myself, I am meant for God.HG

Reflection Questions
In what ways do I delight God?
How is God's redemption being expressed
in and through me?

NO LANGUAGE CAN express the ineffable blessedness of the supreme reward that awaits the soul that has taken its supreme climb, proved its supreme love, and entered on its supreme reward. What an imperturbable certainty there is about the man who is in contact with the real God!NKW

THE LOVE OF God rakes the very bottom of hell, and from the depths of sin and suffering brings sons and daughters to God. To introduce the idea of merit into belief, is to annul my belief and make it blasphemous. Belief requires the renunciation of the idea that I deserve to have things explained to me. When the Spirit of God gets hold of me, He leaves nothing but an aching cavern for God to fill.[HG]

Reflection Questions

How much of my discontent comes from wanting what is not mine? How much of my suffering comes from refusing to discipline my desires?

PEOPLE GO WRONG spiritually because they stubbornly refuse to discipline themselves physically, mentally or in any way, and after a while they become that most contemptible and objectionable thing, and their own greatest cause of suffering. There is no suffering to equal the suffering of self-love arising from independent individuality which refuses to submit either to God or to its nobler self.[NKW]

THE MAINSPRING OF Christ's love for human souls was His love to the Father. If my desire for the salvation of souls is the evangelical commercial craze, may God blast it out of me by the fire of the Holy Ghost. There is such a thing as commercialism in souls as there is in business.ᴵᵀᵂᴮᴾ

Reflection Questions

Is my testimony based on a paltry experience or on a life blazing with an amazing desire, planted there by the Holy Ghost, for God to glorify Himself? ᴵᵀᵂᴮᴾ

THE SUPREME MOMENT of the Cross in actual history is but the concentrated essence of the very nature of the Divine love. God lays down His life for the very creation which men utilize for their own selfish ends. The Self-expenditure of the love of God exhibited in the life and death of our Lord becomes a bridge over the gulf of sin; whereby human love can be imbued by Divine love, the love that never fails.ᴼᴮᴴ

NEVER LOOK FOR other people to be holy; it is a cruel thing to do, it distorts your view of yourself and of others. Could anyone have had a sterner view of sin than Jesus had, and yet had anyone a more loving, tender patience with the worst of men than He had? All He asks of men is that they acknowledge they are not right, then He will do all the rest.[MFL]

Reflection Questions

How much of my grief is due to unreasonable expectations of other people? How much of God's grief is due to my efforts to do what only He can do in another person's heart and life?

ONE OF THE saddest sights to see is Christians who were true go under. This is where it begins—God brought them under the shadow of His hand, and they said, "This is the devil, I have no business to be in darkness," forgetting that there are things God cannot explain.[NI]

WORK, OR YOU will depart from the love of God. Begin to trace the finger of God and the love of God in the great calamities of earth, and in the calamities that have befallen you. In sweat of brain and spirit, work, agonize at times, to keep yourself in the love of God. It is our wisdom, our happiness, our security to keep ourselves in the love of God. How do I keep myself in any sphere but by using every means to abide in it? If I wish to keep in the spiritual sphere of the love of God I must use the great organ of the spiritual realm, faith. "God loves me"—say it o'er and o'er and o'er, heedless of your feelings that come and go. Do not live at a distance from God, live near Him, delighting yourself in Him. Remove all barriers of selfishness and fear, and plunge into the fathomless love of God.^{LG}

Reflection Questions

What fear keeps me wading in the shallow of God's love? What barrier keeps me from plunging into the depths?

SIN IS A disposition of self-love that rules the life apart from God.^{PS}

Love with all your SOUL

WHENEVER GOD HAS given you a blessing, take time to meditate beside the blessing and offer it back to God in a deliberate ecstasy of worship. God will never allow you to hold a spiritual blessing for yourself; it has to be given back to Him that He may make it a blessing to others. If you hoard it, it will turn to spiritual dry rot. If God has blessed you, erect an altar and give the blessing back to God as a love-gift.NKW

Reflection Questions
What blessing have I received that
I have not used to bless others?

SACRIFICE IS THE exuberant passionate love-gift of the best I have to the one I love best. The best gift the Son of God had was His Holy Manhood, and He gave that as a love-gift to God that He might use it as an Atonement for the world. He poured out His soul unto death, and that is to be the characteristic of our lives. God is at perfect liberty to waste us if He chooses. We are sanctified for one purpose only, that we might sanctify our sanctification and give it to God.MFL

IF YOU TAKE the natural view of the love of God you will become atheistic. If God were love according to our natural view of love He ought never to cause us pain, He ought to allow us to be peaceful; but the first thing God does is to cause us pain and to rouse us wide awake. He comes into our lives with ideals and truths which annoy and sting us and break up our rest, until He brings us to the one point, that it is only moral and spiritual relationships which last.[NI]

Reflection Questions

Am I content with only a physical existence or does my soul thirst for a deeper, more meaningful existence?

GOD LOVES THE man who needs Him. Esau was satisfied with what he was; Jacob wanted more than he was. Esau never saw visions, never wrestled with angels, although God was as near to him as to Jacob. Esau refused to sacrifice anything to the spiritual; he could never think of anything but the present. He was willing to sell the promise of the future for a mess of pottage, and thereby he wronged himself far more than Jacob did.[OPG]

Love with all your SOUL

To KNOW THAT God is love, God is holy, God is near, is pure delight to man in his innocent relationship to God, but a terror extreme since the fall. God can never leave a man until He has burned him as pure as He is Himself. It is God's love that forbids He should let him go.PS

Reflection Questions

Am I delighted or terrified by a love so pure that it wants to make me holy? What impurity am I afraid of losing? Why is impurity precious to me?

LOVE MEANS DELIBERATE self-limitation; we deliberately identify ourselves with the interests of our Lord in everything. The revelation comes home to me that God has loved me to the end of all my meanness and my sin, my self-seeking and my wrong motives; and now this is the corresponding revelation—that I have to love others as God has loved me. God will bring around us any number of people we cannot respect, and we have to exhibit the love of God to them as He has exhibited it to us.OBH

JESUS LOVES THE natural virtues, and yet He refers to them in a way which makes them seem utterly futile. Natural virtues are beautiful in the sight of Jesus, but He knows as none other could know, that they are not promises of what man is going to be, but remnants, "trailing clouds of glory," left in man, and are not of the slightest atom of practical use to him. Jesus Christ told the rich young ruler that he must strip himself of all he possessed, give his manhood to Him and then come and follow Him; in other words he must be re-made entirely.[PS]

Reflection Questions

How does my natural virtue get in the way of God's work of making me into a saint? What is the safe and proper place for natural virtue?

THERE IS A lot of sentimental talk about God forgiving because He is love. The Atonement does not mean that God forgives a sinner and allows him to go on sinning and receiving forgiveness; it means that God saves the sinner and turns him into a saint.[PS]

Love with all your SOUL

IF HUMAN LOVE is always discreet and calculating, never carried beyond itself, it is not true love. The characteristic of love is that it is spontaneous, it bursts up in extraordinary ways; it is never premeditated. The reason Jesus called Mary's act "a good work" was because it was wrought out of spontaneous love to Himself. It was neither useful nor her duty; it was an extravagant act for which no one else saw any occasion. The disciples were indignant. Nowadays we are taken up with our ideas of economy and thrift, and never see that those ideas are not God's ideas. The very nature of God is extravagance. How many sunrises and sunsets does God make?PH

Reflection Questions

Is my love for God calculating or extravagant?
Is His love for me calculating or extravagant?

SPIRITUAL MOODS ARE as sensitive and delicate as the awakenings of early love; the most exquisite thing in the human soul is that early mood of the soul when it first falls in love with the Lord.PH

LOVE HAS TO get to its transfiguration point of being poured out before the Lord, otherwise it will get sordid. If you have got bitter and sour, you will probably find it is because God brought you a blessing and you clutched it for yourself; whereas if you had poured it out unto the Lord, you would have been the sweetest person out of heaven.[PH]

Reflection Questions

In what ways have I hoarded or misused God's expression of love, making it into something of no use, or worse? If the natural condition of hoarded resources is pollution and corrosion, what is a better use for them?

SELF-REGARDING LOVE is part weakness, part selfishness, and part romance; and it is this self-regarding love that so counterfeits the higher love that, to the majority, love is too often looked upon as a weak sentimental thing.[PH]

Love with all your SOUL

JUSTICE AND TRUTH and love and honor are at the back of everything, and God must be all these or nothing. And God has undertaken to make a man as holy as He is Himself. God created the universe for man, and God created man to be master of the life in the earth and sea and sky, and the reason he is not is because he took the law into his own hands, and became master of himself, but of nothing else. Man is a remnant of a former design. In the Conscience of God that design is restored.[SA]

Reflection Questions

Do I trust what Jesus can do for me more than what I can do for myself? What keeps me from allowing Jesus to restore me to God's original design?

BEWARE OF A friendship, or of a religion, or of a personal estimate of things that does not reconcile itself to the fact of sin; that is the way all the disasters in human friendships and in human loves begin, and where the compromises start. Jesus Christ never trusted human nature, but He was never cynical, He trusted absolutely what He could do for human nature.[PH]

IN THE NATURAL life when two people fall in love with one another, the individuality is transfigured because the personalities are merged. Identity is not domination, but oneness between two distinct persons in which neither dominates, but the oneness dominates both. In the natural life if the individuality re-asserts itself, there will be hitches and difficulties, and the same with the spiritual life.[PR]

Reflection Questions

In what ways am I being made one with God? In what ways am I refusing to have my personality transformed? What are the dominating and recurring problems in my life that would be cured if God's love were perfected in me?

WE ARE NOT to be absorbed into God as drops in an ocean, we are to be lifted into perfect oneness with Him until God and the glory of perfected human redemption are transfigured by a mutual love.[PR]

Love with all your SOUL

THERE IS NO pain on earth to equal the pain of wounded self-love. Unrequited love is bad enough, but wounded self-love is the cruelest thing in human life because it shifts the whole foundation of life. The prodigal son had his self-love wounded; he was full of shame and indignation because he had sunk to such a level. A repentant soul is never allowed to remain long without being gripped by the love of God.SHL

Reflection Questions

Have I realized the danger of loving myself wrongly? Do I try to feel loved through self-indulgence or self-sacrifice?

THE SELF-EXPENDITURE of the love of God exhibited in the life and death of our Lord becomes a bridge over the gulf of sin; human love can be imbued by Divine love, the love that never fails.RTR

IT IS EASY to be a fisherman when you have all the enthusiasm of the catch; everybody then wants to be a fisherman. Just as everybody comes in with the shout and the "Hallelujah" when revival signs are abroad; but God is wanting those who through long nights, through difficult days of spiritual toil, have been trying to let down their nets to catch the fish. Oh, the skill, the patience, the gentleness and the endurance that are needed for this passion for souls; a sense that men are perishing won't do it; only one thing will do it, a blazing, passionate devotion to the Lord Jesus Christ, an all-consuming passion. Then there is no night so long, no work so hard and no crowd so difficult, but that love will outlast it all.WG

Reflection Questions
Do I have the kind of love that perseveres even though I see no visible results?

GOD GRANT THAT the Holy Spirit may so invade us with the power of God, that we may begin to comprehend the love of Christ for our souls.SHL

WHEN A MAN falls in love his personality emerges and he enters into relationship with another personality. Love is not anything for me at all; love is the deliberate giving of myself right out to another, the sovereign preference of my person for another person. The idea, I must have this person for myself, is not love, but lust. Lust counterfeits love in the same way that individuality counterfeits personality.SHL

Reflection Questions

In what ways has my personality been transformed by God's love?

A MAN HAS his individuality transfigured when he falls in love. When love or the Spirit of God strikes a man or woman, they are transformed, they no longer insist on their separate individuality. Individuality is transfigured in the mastership of God's purpose in Christ Jesus, and the transfiguring element is love; personal, passionate devotion to Himself, and to others.SA

THE WHOLE HUMAN race was created to glorify God and enjoy Him for ever. Sin has switched the human race on to another tack, but it has not altered God's purpose in the tiniest degree; and when we are born again we are brought into the realization of God's great purpose This is the most joyful realization on earth, and we have to learn to rely on the tremendous creative purpose of God. The love of God, the very nature of God, is introduced into us, and the nature of Almighty God is focused in John 3:16 "God so loved the world."CG

Reflection Questions

How much of my life do I spend engaged in my primary pursuit of glorifying God?

ANY FOOL WILL give up wrongdoing and the devil, if he knows how to do it; but it takes a man in love with Jesus Christ to give up the best he has for Him. Jesus Christ does not demand that I give up the wrong, but the right, the best I have for Him—my right to myself.SA

THE INSPIRATION FOR benevolence and philanthropy springs from God, and God's Book has some stern revelations to make about philanthropy and benevolence. It reveals that they may spring from a totally wrong motive. The inspiration of God does not patch up my natural virtues; He re-makes the whole of my being until we find that "every virtue we possess is His alone." God does not come in and patch up our good works, He puts in the Spirit that was characteristic of Jesus; it is His patience, His love, and His tenderness and gentleness that are exhibited through us.[BP]

Reflection Questions

Is my love for God motivated by the desire to delight God or the duty to please Him?

HUMAN AUTHORITY ALWAYS insists on obedience; Our Lord never does. He makes His standard very clear, and if the relation of the spirit within me is that of love to Him, then I do all He says without any hesitation. If I begin to hesitate and to debate, it is because I love someone else in competition with Him—myself.[SSY]

THE CHRISTIAN LIFE is stamped all through with impossibility. Human nature cannot come anywhere near what Jesus Christ demands, and any rational being facing His demands honestly, says, "It can't be done, apart from a miracle." Exactly. It is not that we take the precepts of the Sermon on the Mount and try to live them out literally, but that as we abide in Christ we live out its precepts unconsciously. Being in the Kingdom, we are fit now to live out its laws, and we obey Jesus Christ's commands because of our love for Him.GW

Reflection Questions

If love for God comes from within, from Christ living in me, why do I so often feel as if I am working to pump up loving feelings?

NO HUMAN BEING can pump up what is not there. The consolation of love is not that of exquisite human understanding, it is the real nature of God holding the individual life in effectual rectitude and effectual communion in the face of anything that may ever come.SSY

THE BIBLE DOES not say that God is loving, but that God is love. The phrase "the lovingkindness of God" is frequently used, but when the nature of God is revealed, the Bible does not say God is a loving Being, it says, "God is love."

The same characteristic is revealed in God the Son, not a love that overlooks sin, but a love the essential nature of which is that it delivers from sin.[BP]

Reflection Questions

Does my definition of love expect that my sin will be overlooked or rooted out? If I am unwilling to have God eliminate my sin, how can I expect to be united with Him in love?

THE MARVEL OF the Redemptive Reality of God is that the worst and the vilest can never get to the bottom of His love. Paul did not say that God separated him to show what a wonderful man He could make of him, but "to reveal His Son in me."[CG]

THE FIRST ADAM, the federal head of the race, swung the race on to the basis of wrath, and Jesus Christ, the Last Adam, swung the human race back on to the basis of love. The terms "in Adam," "in Christ," are not mystical terms, but actual revelations of man's condition. When we are "in Adam" we get down to the desolating desert aspect of life. Take love—the most abiding thing about love is its tragedy; or life, the most desolating thing about life is its climax, death. When we are "in Christ" the whole thing is reversed.ᴴᴳᴹ

Reflection Questions

How much wrath remains in me? What keeps me from allowing God's love to replace it?

LORD, UNTO THEE I come in helplessness, yet in hopefulness inwrought by Thy Spirit, that I might be filled with Thy love, Thy Divine un-egoistic nature, Thy passionate patience, unwounded by personal considerations.ᴷᴳᴰ

IF I WATCH God's dealings with me, I shall find that He gives me a revelation of my own pride and bad motives towards Him, and the realization that He loved me when He could not begin to respect me will send me forth into the world to love others as He loved me. God's love for me is inexhaustible, and His love for me is the basis of my love for others. We have to love where we cannot respect and where we must not respect, and this can only be done on the basis of God's love for us.[OBH]

Reflection Questions

What standards do I set up to make people qualify for my love? Where would I be if God did this to me?

O LORD, I do praise Thee that through Christ Jesus our Lord it is mercy and loving-kindness, graciousness and wonders, all along the way; I would I were more sensitive to Thee and Thy doings, more Christlike in my gratitude.[KGD]

HUMAN LOVE MAY illustrate the Divine, it is not identical with the Divine love because of sin. God's own love is so strange to our natural conceptions that we see no love in it; not until we are awakened by the conviction of our sin and anarchy do we realize God's great love towards us—"while we were yet sinners."PH

Reflection Questions

Do I expect people to overlook my sin to prove their love? Why is this an "unloving" request?

IF GOD OVERLOOKED one sin in me, He would cease to be God. The "repenting" of God in individual cases means that God remains true to His purpose and must mean my condemnation, and my condemnation causes Him grief and agony. It is not that God won't overlook wrong, it is that He cannot, His very love forbids it. When I am saved by God's almighty grace I realize that I am delivered completely from what He has condemned—and that is salvation.OPG

Love with all your SOUL

BY MEANS OF the implicit life of a little child Jesus taught the disciples that unless they became 'as this little child,' they could in no wise enter into the kingdom of heaven. The true child of God is such from an inward principle of life from which the life is ordered by implicit loving devotion, as natural as breathing, and as spontaneous as the life of a little child.[CD]

Reflection Questions
Have I moved from the darkness
of hatred and fear to the light of love
and delight? What keeps me from
loving God like a trusting child?

THERE IS NO such thing as being neutral, we are either children of God or of the devil; we either love or we hate; the twilight is torn away ruthlessly.[HGM]

THE JUDGMENTS OF God leave scars, and the scars remain until I humbly and joyfully recognize that the judgments are deserved and that God is justified in them. The last delusion God delivers us from is the idea that we don't deserve what we get. Once we see ourselves under the canopy of God's overflowing mercy we are dissolved in wonder, love and praise.CHI

Reflection Questions
Do I honestly look at what I am like
so that I can clearly see how God's
love has rescued me?

THANK GOD FOR the deep profound note of the glorious Gospel of God, that Jesus Christ as Savior can justify ungodly men, can set them free from their sin; and as Sanctifier He can make them into sons and daughters of God, able to love others as God has loved them, able to show others the same unconditioned mercy He has showed them.GW

THE NATURE OF the faith born in me by the Holy Ghost will take me back to the Source and enable me to see what God is like, and until I am all light and all love in Him, the things in me which are not of that character will have to pass.CHI

Reflection Questions
Have my acts of faith been transformed
into deeds of love?

WE DISCERN NOT by faith, but by love, by intimacy with God. The Old Testament makes much of faith; the New Testament makes everything of the relationship of love; That is why our Lord placed Mary of Bethany's act so high; it was not an act of faith, but of absolute love. The breaking of the alabaster box revealed the unconscious sympathy of her spirit with Jesus Christ.HGM

ONE OF THE most remarkable things about Jesus Christ is that although He was full of love and gentleness, yet in His presence every one not only felt benefited, but ashamed. It is His presence that judges us; we long to meet Him, and yet we dread to.ᴴᴳᴹ

Reflection Questions

In what ways has my fear of God faded as my love for Him has grown? Am I more motivated by the fear of His wrath or the delight of His love?

THE FELLOWSHIP OF the disciples is based not on natural affinities of taste but on fellowship in the Holy Ghost, a fellowship that is constrained and enthralled by the love and communion of our Lord and Savior Jesus Christ. When both sides of this fellowship, listening in darkness and speaking in light, are realized, no darkness can terrify any more.ᴾᴴ

THE LOVE OF God is not revealed by intellectual discernment, it is a spiritual revelation. What ups and downs we experience because we build not on faith but on feeling, not on the finished work of Christ but on our own work and endeavor and experience.[LG]

Reflection Questions

If I resist giving up something bad,
how can I expect to receive anything good?

IF YOU ONLY give up wrong things for Jesus Christ, don't talk any more about being in love with Him. We say, "Why shouldn't I? It isn't wrong!" What a sordid thing to say! When we love a person, do we only give up what is wrong for him? Love is not measured by what it gets, but by what it costs, and our relationship to Jesus Christ can never be on the line of, "Why shouldn't I do this?"[PR]

95

WHEN WE RECEIVE the nature of God into us, the first thing that happens is that God takes away all pretence and pious pose; and He does it by revealing that He loved us, not because we were loveable, but because it is His nature to love. God is love.ᴼᴮᴴ

Reflection Questions
Do I see in others their potential in Christ?
Do I even look for it?

LOVE IS NOT blind; love sees a great deal more than the actual. If you love someone you are not blind to his defects but you see the ideal which exactly fits that one. God sees all our crudities and defects, but He also sees the ideal for us; He sees "every man perfect in Christ Jesus," consequently He is infinitely patient.ᴼᴾᴳ

Love

with all your MIND

NEVER LET ANYTHING push you to your wits' end, because you will worry, and worry makes you self-interested and disturbs the nourishment of the life of God. Give thanks to God that He is there, no matter what is happening. The secret of Christian quietness is not indifference, but the knowledge that God is my Father, He loves me, I shall never think of anything He will forget. Then worry becomes an impossibility.[IYA]

Reflection Questions

What do I worry about that I think God has forgotten? If I worry that I will be misunderstood, what am I forgetting?

WE HAVE TO get rid of the idea that we are going to be vindicated down here; Jesus was not. The triumphant thing for a saint is to stand true to God in spite of all the odds the world, the flesh and the devil can bring. God's Spirit will lead us away from our limitations and teach us to think the thoughts of God behind the things that contradict them. At the back of all is the love of God which will not let a soul go. If you are a servant of God, He will put you through desert experiences without asking your permission.[NI]

Love with all your MIND

THE CHARACTERISTICS OF man's union with God are faith in God and love for Him. This union was the first thing Satan aimed at in Adam and Eve, and he did it by perverting what God had said. In the case of Job, Satan goes the length of trying to pervert God's idea of man. That is an amazing revelation of the power of Satan! He is represented as presenting himself with the sons of God in the very presence of God and trying to pervert God's mind about Job.[BP]

Reflection Questions

In what ways has Satan tried to corrupt my thinking about God and His love? In what ways has he been successful? What must occur to keep me from being deceived?

WHEN WE ARE tied up with other people's notions of what we should be, the only way to get rid of it all is to take this plunge into the love of God. We have to form the mind of Christ until we are absorbed in Him and take no account of the evil done to us. No love on earth can do this but the love of God.[ITWBP]

To THINK AS a Christian is a rare accomplishment, especially as the curious leaven which puts a premium on ignorance works its sluggish way. A blatant pride which boasts of knowing nothing outside the Bible, in all probability, knows nothing inside it either. Christian thinking is a rare and difficult thing; so many seem unaware that the first great commandment according to our Lord is, "Thou shalt love the Lord thy God . . . with all thy mind. . . ."CG

Reflection Questions

In what ways do I engage my mind in acts of love and worship? What "fear of knowing" keeps me from thinking?

MANY A CHRISTIAN who loves Jesus Christ in his heart denies Him in his head.BSG

IT IS ONLY by getting our mind into the state of the Mind of Jesus that we can understand how it is possible to fulfill the royal law and love our neighbor as ourselves. We measure our generosity by the standards of men; Jesus says, "Measure your love for men by God's love for them, and if you are My disciple, you will love your neighbor as I have loved you."CHI

Reflection Questions

In what ways would my love be more compelling if I agreed with God about what is good? In what ways would my testimony be more convincing if my mind and heart were in agreement with God?

HOW MUCH OF faith, hope, and love is worked in us when we try to convince somebody else? It is not our business to convince other people, that is the insistence of a merely intellectual, unspiritual life. The Spirit of God will do the convicting when we are in the relationship where we simply convey God's word.ITWBP

WATCH THE MARGINS of your mind when you begin to take the view that it doesn't matter whether God is holy or not; it is the beginning of being a traitor to Jesus Christ. Spiritual insight does not so much enable us to understand God as to understand that He is at work in the ordinary things of life, in the ordinary stuff human nature is made of.[DI]

Reflection Questions

Am I becoming more and more in love with God as a holy God, or with the conception of an amiable Being who says, "Oh well, sin doesn't matter much"?

IF MY WORSHIP is consumed in the glory of the Lord till that is the one thing left in my mind, I have come to the right place of vision. Anything that belittles or obliterates the holiness of God by a false view of the love of God is untrue to the revelation given by Jesus Christ.[NI]

Love with all your MIND

THE SPIRIT OF God corrupts our natural virtues. If we are naturally pure-minded, good-tempered, loving, we shall find that since we became spiritual God's corruption has been put on everything that was of old, because the natural virtues are not promises of what we are going to be, but remnants of what we were created to be, and the new life re-forms its own virtues. It is the most woeful thing to see people in the service of God depending on what they have by the accidents of heredity. Intellectually we nearly always sympathize with pagan virtues, while spiritually God is trying to get us into contact with the real life of the Lord Jesus Christ that cannot be described in terms of natural virtues.ᴺᴶ

Reflection Questions
In what ways is God reforming my natural
virtues to make them instruments
of love and worship?

THE BIBLE RECORDS that "God is love"; but it must be borne in mind that it is the love of God, and that love is inexpressible bliss to a Being like Jesus Christ, or to a being like Adam as God created him.ᴾˢ

103

GOD IS LOVE. No one but God could have revealed that to the world, for we see nothing but its contradiction in our own limited experience. From shattered, broken lives, from caverns of despair, comes the contradiction to any such statement. No wonder the carnal mind, the merely intellectually cultured, consider us infatuated, mere dreamers, talking of love when murder and war and famine and lust and pestilence, and all the refinement of selfish cruelty is abroad in the earth. But, oh the sublimity of the Abraham-like faith that dares to place the center of its life and confidence and action and hope in an unseen and apparently unknown God, saying, "God is love," in spite of all appearances to the contrary.[LG]

Reflection Questions

In what ways has the mind of Christ been formed in me so that I can see the good that God has in mind rather than the evil that man conceives?

WE HAVE TO form the mind of Christ until we are absorbed with Him and take no account of the evil done to us. No love on earth can do this but only the love of God.[RTR]

WORDS AND EMOTIONS pass, precious as their influence may be for the time, so when the duller moments come and the mind comes to require something more certain and sure to consider than the memory of mere emotions and stirring sentiments—consider this revelation, the eternal fact that God is Love. God and love are synonymous. Love is not an attribute of God, it is God; whatever God is, love is.[LG]

Reflection Questions

*In what ways have I made truth clear
by walking in obedience? What error
in thinking causes me to stumble?*

THE TRUTH ABOUT God is Jesus Christ—light, life, and love. Whatever is dark to us will, by means of our obedience, become as clear as the truth which we have made ours by obedience. The bit we do know is the most glorious, unfathomable delight conceivable, and that is going to be true about everything to do with God and us.[NJ]

WHEN GOD IS revealed as Love, as Holy, and as Near, it is man's conscience that alarms him from his sleep of death; it makes hell for a man instead of a life of peace. Wherever Jesus comes He reveals that man is away from God by reason of sin, and he is terrified at His presence. That is why men will put anything in the place of Jesus Christ, anything rather than let God come near in His startling purity, because immediately God comes near, conscience records that God is holy and nothing unholy can live with Him, consequently His presence hurts the sinner.PS

Reflection Questions

Has my conscience been aligned with God in such a way that it guides me away from sin? Or does my conscience still lure me away from God?

I WOULD, O Lord, have all my thought and emotions and words redolent with love, perfect love to Thee, and through that to men.KGD

ALWAYS DISTINGUISH between warning and threatening. God never threatens; the devil never warns. A warning is a great arresting statement of God's, inspired by His love and patience. This throws a flood of light on the vivid statements of Jesus Christ, such as "How can ye escape the damnation of hell?" There is no element of personal vindictiveness. Be careful how you picture our Lord when you read His terrible utterances. Read His denunciations with Calvary in your mind.SSM

Reflection Questions

Am I grateful or resentful of God's warnings?
Do I consider them an act of loving concern or
mean-spirited meddling? Would the world be
better or worse without warnings of
the dangers of sin?

O LORD, FOR more love, passionate, devout and earnest love to Thee to show itself in my conscious life. Oh for grace to show and to feel patience and gentleness to those around me!KGD

THE MOTIVE AT the back of the precepts of the Sermon on the Mount is love of God. Read the Beatitudes with your mind fixed on God, and you will realize their neglected side. Their meaning in relationship to men is so obvious that it scarcely needs stating, but the Godward aspect is not so obvious. "Blessed are the poor in spirit"—towards God.ˢˢᴹ

Reflection Questions

*Am I a pauper towards God? Do I know that I cannot prevail in prayer; that I cannot blot out the sins of the past; that I cannot alter my disposition; and that I cannot lift myself nearer to God?*ˢˢᴹ

LORD, CAUSE THY loving-kindness to be known by me this day by Thine inevitably powerful touches, and use me in Thy gentle almightiness for Thy purposes.ᴷᴳᴰ

IF OUR IDEA is that we are being mastered, it is a proof that we have no master; if that is our attitude to Jesus, we are far away from the relationship He wants. He wants us in the relationship in which He is easily Master without our conscious knowledge of it, all we know is that we are His to obey.^{CG}

Reflection Questions

Does my relationship with God require effort? Am I often exhausted from doing good? What does this say about who I am trusting?

IF WE ONLY take as answers those that are visible to our senses, we are in a very elemental condition of grace. Can it be said of us that Jesus so loved us that He stayed where He was because He knew we had a capacity to stand a bigger revelation? Has God trusted us with a silence, a silence that is absolutely big with meaning? That is His answer. The manifestation will come in a way beyond any possibility of comprehension.^{IYA}

THINK OF THE things you prayed to God about and tried to hold and, because of His love, He dare not let you hold them and they went. You prayed that you might keep the thing that seemed to make your life as a Christian possible, and suddenly the whole thing went to pieces. That was God's answer. If we are spiritual and can interpret His silence, we always get the trust in God that knows prayers are answered every time, not sometimes.[IYA]

Reflection Questions
What have I asked for and not received?
What have I received instead?

IF GOD IS taking us into the understanding that prayer is for the glorifying of His Father, He will give us the first sign of His intimacy—silence. The devil calls it unanswered prayer; in the case of Martha and Mary the Spirit of God called it a sign that He loved them, and because He loved them and knew they were fit to receive a bigger revelation than ever they dreamed of, He stayed where He was. His silence is the sign that He is bringing us into this marvelous understanding of Himself.[IYA]

WHEN GOD STOPS giving us things, He brings us into the place where we can begin to understand Him. As long as we get from God everything we ask for, we never get to know Him, we look upon Him as a bless-ing-machine, that has nothing to do with God's char-acter or with our characters. It is not sufficient for us to say, "Oh yes, God is love." We have to know He is love. We have to struggle through until we do see He is love and justice. Then our prayer is answered.[IYA]

Reflection Questions

What need do I have that God might be meeting in a way that I'm not expecting? How many expectations keep me from seeing the bigger picture of what God is doing and how He is working to give me something more, though perhaps different, than I have asked?

THE CROSS OF Christ reveals that the blazing center of the love of God is the holiness of God, not His kind-ness and compassion.[PH]

THE ONLY BIT of God we understand is the bit we have obeyed. To the intellect it is absurd to call God loving and just, but immediately you obey God you begin to discern that God is a God of absolute love and justice. The discernment is a satisfaction not to your intellect but to your life. Never be surprised if there are whole areas of thinking that are not clear; they never will be until you obey (John 7:17).[NJ]

Reflection Questions

Do I demand to understand before being obedient? If knowing is really important to me, why would I continue to disobey if obedience leads to understanding?

THE PRESENTATION OF the Gospel of God to sinners is one of love and mercy, but to the house of God one of judgment and truth. When we preach to the crowd outside we lambaste drunkenness and other things. Jesus never did. The stern messages of the Bible are never given to sinners, but to God's people. If we follow the order God gives, we will not go astray.[NJ]

THERE ARE PEOPLE whose lives are diseased and twisted by a sense of duty which God never inspired; but once let them begin to think about the things of loveliness, and the healing forces that will come into their lives will be amazing. The very essence of godliness is in the things of loveliness; think about these things, says Paul.[MFL]

Reflection Questions

Do I make room for beauty in my thinking or do I consider it wasteful? Am I so focused on what is true and right that I neglect what is lovely?

SOME EXCEPTIONALLY GIFTED men may derive their conception of God from other sources than the Bible. But all I know of God I have got from the Bible. In all my dreams and imaginings and visions I see God, but it is the God of the Bible that I see. I see ever amid the mysteries of Providence and Grace and Creation "a Face like my face," and "a Hand like this hand," and I have learned to love God Who gave me such a sure way of knowing Him and left me not to the vain imaginations of my own sin-warped intellect.[LG]

To TRACE THAT God is love by mere unaided human intellect. But it is not impossible to the intuitions of faith. Lift up your eyes and look abroad over the whole earth, and in the administration of God's moral government you will begin to discern that God is love, that over sin and war and death and hell He reigns supreme, that His purposes are ripening fast. We must by holy contemplation of all we have considered keep ourselves in the love of God, then we shall not be able to despond for long.[LG]

Reflection Questions

Is my understanding of God based on what man does to creation or on what the Bible says creation tells me about God?

GOD IS LOVE — one brief sentence, you can print it on a ring: it is the Gospel. A time is coming when the whole round world will know that God reigns and that God is Love, when hell and heaven, life and death, sin and salvation, will be read and understood aright at last.[LG]

Love with all your MIND

THE LOVE OF God! We have lost it today; we have turned our back on the ocean and are looking out over barren colorless hills for the ocean's fullness. We need converting again—turning round, and there basks the ocean's fullness, whose waves sparkle and ripple on fathomless deeps and fullnesses. We are too introspective today, we mourn and wonder, then lifted on waves of feeling, we glow and say we love God, but again our feelings ebb and flow and we mourn.[LG]

Reflection Questions

Is my love for God based on how I feel about Him or what I know about Him? Do I doubt God when He takes me places that don't appear on my handmade life journey map?

WHEN GOD CALLS us He does not tell us what to expect; God's call is a command that asks us, that means there is always a possibility of refusal on our part. Faith never knows where it is being led, it knows and loves the One Who is leading. It is a life of faith, not of intelligence and reason, but a life of knowing Who is making me "go."[NKW]

IN THE GENERALITY of our days our love for God is too deeply imbedded to be conscious; it is neither joy nor peace, it is "me" obsessed by God in the unconscious domain. Love, to be love, is deeper than I am conscious of, and is only revealed by crises. This intense personal love is the only kind of love there is.[BP]

Reflection Questions

Are my thoughts about God based on my limited experiences or on God's unlimited revelation? What am I to do with thoughts that don't fit the definition that God is love?

WHEN ALL RELIGIONS and philosophies and philologies have tried to define God, one and all sink inane and pass, while the Bible statements stand like eternal monuments, shrouded in ineffable glory: "GOD IS LIGHT"; "GOD IS LOVE"; "GOD IS HOLY." Every attempted definition of God other than these sublime inspirations negates God, and we find ourselves possessed of our own ideas with never a glimpse of the living God.[CD]

IF YOU HAVE never felt inclined to call God cruel and hard, it is a question whether you have ever faced any problems at all. Job's utterances are those of a man who suffers without any inkling as to why he suffers; yet he discerns intuitively that what is happening to him is not in God's order, although it is in His permissive will. All through, Job stands for two things: that God is just, and that he is relatively innocent. Remember, Job was never told the preface to his own story; he did not know that he had been chosen to be the battleground between God and Satan. Satan's contention was that no man loved God for His own sake.CHI

Reflection Questions

Would I still love God if He took away every indication that He loves me? If God is love, and if the nature of love is to give, what might God be giving me by taking away something I already have?

THE NATURE OF love is to give, not to receive.OPG

IT IS NOT faith to believe that God is making things work together for good unless we are up against things that are ostensibly working for bad. God's order does come in the haphazard, but only to those who love God. The only way in which God's order is recognized in our lives is by being what Jesus calls "born from above." God's order comes to us in the ordinary haphazard circumstances of life, and when we are in touch with Him the sacrament of His presence comes in the common elements of Nature and ordinary people.[HGM]

Reflection Questions

In what ways does my obsession with order get in the way of my passion for the Lord?

THE MAJORITY OF us have a bloodless idea, an impersonal, ethereal, vague abstraction, called "love to God." Jesus mentions relationships of the closest, most personal, most passionate order, and says that our love for Him must be closer and more personal than any of those (see Luke 14:26).[ITWBP]

THE REASON THE desert came is that man ate of the fruit of the tree of knowledge of good and evil. God placed the tree in the garden, but He did not intend that man should eat of its fruit; He intended man to know evil only by contrast with good, as Our Lord did. The man who knows good by contrast with evil shall find life a desolating desert. When the cosmic order of earth and the moral nature of man are in touch with God, the order of the earth is beauty, and the order of human life is love. Immediately a man gets out of touch with God, he finds the basis of things is not beauty and love, but chaos and wrath.[HGM]

Reflection Questions

What knowledge of evil has become part of my way of thinking? Would the world be better or worse if we knew more about good than evil? Why am I so curious about evil?

THE CURIOUS THING about the love of God is that it is the cruelest thing on earth to everything that is not of Him. God hurts desperately when I am far away from Him; but when I am close to Him, He is unutterably tender.[OBH]

THE REALIZATION OF the nature of God's love produces in me the convulsions of repentance, and repentance fully worked out means holiness, a radical adjustment of the life. Do I know God has saved me? Have I the satisfaction of that salvation? I can easily know whether the Redemption has been made efficacious in me by the Holy Spirit by the fact that I am at one with God. The Redemption is worked out in an at-one-ment with God, in every calculation He is the One Who dominates everything.[HG]

Reflection Questions

Has the revelation of God's love caused me to repent? From what sins have I turned away? Which ones continue to lure me away and keep me from being united with God and with other believers?

WE SAY WE believe that God is love, but have we learned that He is? Have we assimilated it? We see truths, but we are not yet in the circumstances where we can learn them. Many things are taught, but we cannot learn them all at once.[OBH]

Love with all your MIND

LOVE, MORE THAN any other experience in life, reveals the shallowness and the profundity, the hypocrisy and the nobility, of human nature. In dealing with all implicit things, such as love, there is a danger of being sentimentally consistent to a doctrine or an idea while the actual life is ignored; we forget that we have to live in this world as human beings. Consistency in doctrine ought to work out into expression in actual life.ᴼᴾᴳ

Reflection Questions

In what ways does doctrine make me a better lover of God and others? Am I content with the knowledge of God or do I crave other knowledge? Do I think that love and truth can exist apart from God?

GOD WANTS TO get us out of the love of virtue and in love with the God of virtue—stripped of all possessions but our knowledge of Him.ᴵᵀᵂᴮᴾ

WHEN WE PREACH the love of God there is a danger of forgetting that the Bible reveals not first the love of God but the intense, blazing holiness of God, with His love as the center of that holiness. When the holiness of God is preached, men are convicted of sin. The awful nature of the conviction of sin that the Holy Spirit brings makes us realize that God cannot, dare not, must not forgive sin; if God forgave sin without atoning for it our sense of justice would be greater than His.^{PS}

Reflection Questions

Do I allow Scripture to form my convictions and reveal my sin, or do I impose my convictions on Scripture to conceal my sin?

THE TROUBLE WITH most of us is that we will walk only in the light of our conviction of what the light is. We have any number of glorious opportunities of proving how much we love God by the delighted way we go to sacrifice for Him.^{ITWBP}

Love with all your MIND

THE RATIONALIST DEMANDS an explanation of everything. The reason I won't have anything to do with God
is because I cannot define Him. If I can define God, I am
greater than the God I define. If I can define love and
life, I am greater than they are. Solomon indicates that
there is a great deal we do not know and cannot define.
We have to go on trust in a number of ways, therefore,
he says, be careful that you are not too emphatic and
dogmatic in your exposition of things.SHH

Reflection Questions

*In what ways do I trust my own understanding
of the world more than God's explanation of
it? If God's explanation is right, what attitudes
and actions must I change to agree with it?*

THERE IS NO problem, no personal grief, no agony or
distress (and God knows there are some fathomless
agonies—awful injustices and wrongs and evils and nobility all mixed up together) but will have an overwhelming explanation one day. If we will hang in to the fact
that God is true and loving and just, every judgment He
passes will find us in agreement with it finally.SHH

THE PRODIGAL REMEMBERED his Father when he had spent all. He should have remembered him, gratefully, and with increasing understanding of his love and care, when his Father was bestowing on him his goods. God gives us all things richly to enjoy, and in youth and early manhood heaps rich precious bounties upon us, God must be remembered then, else we shall grievously hurt Him, and defraud ourselves.SHH

Reflection Questions

Am I able to learn from good things or just from bad experiences? What lessons would be less painful if I were more attentive to God when life is going well?

NOT UNTIL WE realize that there is something tragic at the basis of human life shall we recognize the love of God.PH

THE FIRST THING we need to be educated in spiritually is a knowledge of the dimensions of Divine love, its length and depth and breadth and height. That God is love is a revelation. Unless I am born from above, what is the use of telling me God is love? To me He is not love. No one who faces facts as they are could ever prove that God is love unless he accepts the revelation of His love made by Jesus Christ.[PH]

Reflection Questions

What proof do I need before I will believe that God is good? What evidence am I demanding that God has not provided?

THE CROSS OF Jesus is the supreme evidence of the love of God.[PH]

THESE ARE SOME of the lines of spiritual education: learning the dimensions of Divine Love, that the center of that love is holiness; that the direction of Divine living is a deliberate surrender of our own point of view in order to learn Jesus Christ's point of view, and seeing that men and women are nourished in the knowledge of Jesus.PH

Reflection Questions

How much time and energy do I spend trying to get others to agree with me rather than with God?

IF YOU LOVE Me, says Jesus, "Feed My sheep." "Don't make converts to your way of thinking, but look after My sheep, see that they are nourished in the knowledge of Me."PH

ONE OF THE last lessons we learn is not to be an amateur providence—"I shall not allow that person to suffer." Suffering, and the inevitable result of suffering, is the only way some of us can learn, and if we are shielded God will ultimately take the one who interferes by the scruff of the neck and remove him. The fingers that caress a child may also hurt its flesh; it is the power of love that makes them hurt.SHH

Reflection Questions
In what ways have I been hurt
because I insist on learning from experience
rather than from instruction?

FAITH FOR MY deliverance is not faith in God. Faith means, whether I am visibly delivered or not, I will stick to my belief that God is love. There are some things only learned in a fiery furnace.RTR

127

THE DISPOSITION RULING within me determines the way I interpret outside things. A man convicted of sin and a man in love may live in the same external world, but in totally different creations. Both may be in the desert, but the disposition of the one makes him interpret the desert as a desolating piece of God's territory; while to the other the desert literally blossoms as the rose.[SA]

Reflection Questions

How is my own spiritual condition affecting the way I see the world? Do I see love and hope or hate and futility? What does my point of view tell me about my position in Christ?

WE CAN CHANGE the world without when we change the recording instrument within. Commit sin, and I defy you to see anything beautiful without; fall in love, and you will see beauty in everything.[SA]

SOMEONE HAS DONE us a wrong, and we say, "Now I must be careful. . . ." Our attitude is to be that of the expressed love of God, and if we take the evil into account we cannot express His love. We must deal with that one as God has dealt with us. There is no bigger, stiffer job for a saint than that.SHL

Reflection Questions

Who does Christ want to love through me?
What injustice done to me has made me overly
cautious? How might undue caution keep me
from fulfilling the high calling of God:
to love others as He loves me?

WE HAVE TO love where we cannot respect and where we must not respect, and this can only be done on the basis of God's love for us.RTR

THE JUDGMENTS OF God are a consuming fire whereby He destroys in order to deliver; the time to be alarmed in life is when all things are undisturbed. The knowledge that God is a consuming fire is the greatest comfort to the saint, it is His love at work on those characteristics that are not true to godliness. The saint who is near to God knows no burning, but the farther away from God the sinner gets, the more the fire of God burns him.CHI

Reflection Questions
What evidence does my life reveal that God is at work in me? What evidence do others see that God loves me?

WHEN A MAN does love his enemies, he knows that God has done a tremendous work in him, and every one else knows it too.SSM

A FALSE IDEA of God's honor ends in misinterpreting His ways. It is the orthodox type of Christian who by sticking to a crude idea of God's character, presents the teaching which says, "God loves you when you are good, but not when you are bad." God loves us whether we are good or bad. That is the marvel of His love.[CHI]

$\mathcal{R}$eflection $\mathcal{Q}$uestions

What fundamental change in my thinking is required for me to believe that God loves sinners? What can love accomplish that faulty human conceptions of truth and justice cannot?

JESUS CHRIST'S STATEMENTS reveal that God is a Being of love and justice and truth; the actual happenings in our immediate circumstances seem to prove He is not; are we going to remain true to the revelation that God is good?[SSM]

WHEN WE CONSIDER the life of our Lord Jesus Christ, [we] notice that His first obedience was to the will of His Father, not to the needs of humanity. It is a difficult matter to adjust the relationship of these two callings, but the delicate adjustment is brought about by the Spirit of God, for the Spirit and the Word of God ever put first things first, and the first thing is love to God and obedience to God, and the second, service to humanity.^{CD}

Reflection Questions

In what ways do I mistake my expressions of charity to others as acts of love to God? In what ways has my love for others become a substitute for love for God?

VERY FEW OF us know what _love of God_ is, we know what _love of moral good_ is, and the curious thing is that that leads us away from God more quickly than does a terror of moral evil; "the good is ever the enemy of the best."^{DI}

Love with all your MIND

IF YOUR CONCEPTION of love does not agree with justice and judgment and purity and holiness, then your idea of love is wrong. It is not love you conceive of in your mind, but some vague infinite foolishness, all tears and softness and of infinite weakness.[LG]

Reflection Questions

How does my vague notion of love conflict with the love of God that is holy and pure? How has my own common sense led me astray?

IF IN A crisis we act according to common sense we do not express the love of God.[SHL]

WE GET THE idea that wrong views of God and of goodness arise from a life that is wrong; the Bible shows that wrong views of God and of goodness may arise out of a life that is right. The parable of the two sons is an example of this. The younger brother was a wastrel; the elder brother was a man of integrity, but he made the fatal error of misinterpreting his father's ways and refusing to enter into a love that was too big for this earth.CHI

Reflection Questions

In what ways does my own self-perceived goodness get in the way of God's righteousness? Is love an aspect of my life or my entire disposition?

MANY GOOD UPRIGHT people misinterpret God's ways because they do not take into account first of all the matter of personal relationship to God. They say because we are the creatures of God, we are the sons and daughters of God; Jesus Christ taught with profound insistence that we are sons and daughters of God only by an inner disposition, the disposition of love.CHI

THE BIBLE STATES that "love is of God." The difficulty arises out of our individuality, which keeps us segregated from others. The attitude of the elder brother is individual entirely, he is merged into nothing of the nature of love, consequently he misunderstands his father and demands that his ways ought to be more clearly justifiable to human reason. God's ways never are, because the basis of things fundamentally is not reasonable. Our reason is simply an instrument, the way we explain things, it is not the basis of things.[CHI]

Reflection Questions

In what ways does individuality keep me from experiencing and expressing the love of God?

THE PROBLEMS OF life are only explainable by means of a right relationship to God. If we ask for a reasonable explanation of God's ways, we will end up misinterpreting God; but when we receive the loving disposition Jesus Christ came to give us, we find our problems are explained implicitly.[CHI]

NATURALLY, WE DO not love God; we mistrust Him. Consequently in thinking we are apt to apply to God what should be applied to Satan. Satan uses the problems of this life to slander God's character; he tries to make us think that all the calamities and miseries and wrongs spring from God.[BP]

Reflection Questions

What problem or difficulty do I attribute to God rather than Satan? In what ways is my thinking not yet aligned with Jesus?

UNTIL A MAN is born again his thinking goes in a circle and he becomes intoxicated with his own importance. When he is born again there is a violent readjustment in his actual life, and when he begins to think along Jesus Christ's line there is just as tremendous a revolution in his thinking processes. To bring every thought into captivity is the last thing we do, and it is not done easily; in the beginning we have to do violence to our old ways of thinking just as at sanctification we had to do violence to our old ways of living. Intellect in a saint is the last thing to become identified with Jesus Christ.[BSG]

Love
with all your STRENGTH

THE REALIZATION THAT my strength is always a hindrance to God's supply of life is a great eye-opener. A man who has genius is apt to rely on his genius rather than on God. A man who has money is apt to rely on money instead of God. So many of us trust in what we have got in the way of possessions instead of entirely in God. All these sources of strength are sources of double weakness. But when we realize that our true life is "hid with Christ in God," that we are "complete in Him," then His strength is radiantly manifested in our mortal flesh, and His light and life and love shine more and more unto the perfect day.ᴳᵂ

Reflection Questions

What natural ability do I have that is weakness masquerading as strength because it keeps me relying on my own strength rather than on God?

THE GODS OF other religions are unmoved by men's troubles simply because they do not care; but our God in His love and compassion imposes on Himself our weakness and pain, while yet He is unmoved from the well-centered strength of His mighty purposes.ᶜᴰ

THE NATURAL LIFE in a sanctified man or woman is neither moral nor immoral; it is the gift God has given to be sacrificed on the altar of love to God. Jesus Christ had a natural body, it was not a sin for Him to be hungry, but it would have been a sin for Him to satisfy that hunger when God had told Him not to. The body we have is not sinful in itself; if it were, it would be untrue to say that Jesus Christ was sinless. After we are sanctified we have the same body, but it is ruled by a new disposition, and we have to sacrifice our natural life to God even as Jesus did, so that we make the natural life spiritual by a series of direct moral choices.ITWBP

Reflection Questions
In what way do my choices indicate
that my natural life is being made spiritual
through the love of God?

THE SAINT HAS one striking characteristic, and that is in loving with a Divine love. Its thirst is not so much to be loved as to be lovable. The characteristics in the life of the saint are the characteristics of our Lord's life. The saint bears a strong family likeness to Jesus Christ.CD

It is His perfections, not ours; His patience, His love, His holiness, His strength. There is a danger with the children of God of getting too familiar with sublime things. We talk so much about these wonderful realities, and forget that we have to exhibit them in our lives. It is perilously possible to mistake the exposition of the truth for the truth; to run away with the idea that because we are able to expound these things we are living them too. OBH

Reflection Questions

In what ways do my wonderful ideas about God keep me from allowing Him to do wonderful things in me? How do love, joy, peace, and other fruits of the Spirit make me strong in Christ?

In DAYS GONE by we all used to love the creatures that exhibit reflections of the Eternal Good—honor and courage and strength, but when we are made one with Jesus Christ we find we love the creatures that exhibit the fruit of the Spirit. ITWBP

THE DEATH OF Jesus not only gives us remission from our sins, it enables us to assimilate the very nature of Jesus until in every detail of our lives we are like Him. How much more does the death of Jesus mean to us today than it ever has before? Are we beginning to be lost in wonder, love and praise at the marvellous loosening from sin, and are we so assimilating the nature of Jesus that we bear a strong family likeness to Him?[PS]

Reflection Questions

*Am I lost in wonder, love, and praise
or still lost in self-centered sin? Am I eager
to have Christ's likeness seen in me
or would I rather be left alone?*

"IF ONLY GOD would leave me alone!" men are apt to cry. God never will. His passionate, inexorable love never allows Him to leave men alone, and with His children He will shake everything that can be shaken till nothing more can be shaken; then will abide the consuming fire of God until the life is changed into the same image from glory to glory.[OBH]

"ANGUISH" COMES FROM a word meaning to press tightly, to strangle, and the idea is not a bit too strong for the things people are going through. They are not sentimental things, but real things, where every bit of a man's life is twisted and wrung out to the last ebb. Can the love of God in Christ hold there, when everything says that God is cruel to allow it, and that there is no such thing as justice and goodness? Shall anguish separate us from the love of God? No, we are more than conquerors in it, not by our own effort but by the fact that the love of God in Christ holds.SHL

Reflection Questions

In what ways has going through times of anguish made me stronger? How have the weapons Satan used to make me weaker made me stronger instead?

THE LOVE OF God in Christ Jesus is such that He can take the most unfit man—unfit to survive, unfit to fight, unfit to face moral issues—and make him not only fit to survive and to fight, but fit to face the biggest moral issues and the strongest power of Satan, and come off more than conqueror.RTR

THE MOST PAINFUL and most crushing thing to a man or woman is unrequited love. In summing up the attitude of men to Himself, God says that that is the way men treat Him, they "un-requite" His love. It is only when we come to our wits' ends, or reap a distress, or feel the first twinge of damnation and are knocked out of our complacent mental agility over things, that we recognize the love of God.ᔆᴴᴴ

Reflection Questions

What habits do I have that cultivate the love of Christ in me? In what ways do I practice love? What loss of love compels me to take refuge in God's love?

NEITHER NATURAL LOVE nor Divine love will remain unless it is cultivated. We must form the habit of love until it is the practice of our lives.ᴼᴮᴴ

THE PRODUCTION OF saints, that is the work. God Almighty regenerates men's souls; we make disciples. Are we doing it? God is apparently not very careful whom or what He uses for the work of regeneration; but none but saints can make disciples. God's curse is on the spiritual nature that cannot reproduce its own kind.CD

Reflection Questions

Does my work for God stamp the hearts of the people around me with an enervating, sentimental love for me? Or does every remembrance of me cause a stirring of hearts to do better, grander work for God?

LOVE RENDERS IMPOTENT the strength of our most formidable enemy. Any of the elemental ministries—life, death, things present, things to come—may kill the castles built by human love; may remove and shatter them like an incoming tide, their strength is overwhelming, but they are powerless to touch the love of God in Christ Jesus.SHL

Love with all your STRENGTH

THE OUTWARD IS the symbol of the inner, according to the Bible. There is a closer connection between them than we imagine. When our supreme temptation comes, the setting we are in, whether it is a city or the actual desert, brings us into contact with the foundation of things as God made them. According to Genesis, the basis of physical material life is chaos, and the basis of personal moral life, wrath. If I live in harmony with God, chaos becomes cosmos to me, and the wrath of God becomes the love of God.ᴴᴳᴹ

Reflection Questions

What evidence do I see that the love of God is overcoming chaos and wrath in my life? Do I find strength in the joy of the Lord?

WHEN WE KNOW the love of Christ, which passeth knowledge, it means we are free from anxiety, free from carefulness, so that, during the twenty-four hours of the day, we do what we ought to do all the time, with the strength of life bubbling up with real spontaneous joy.ᴿᵀᴿ

145

PAUL SAYS HE is overruled, overmastered, held as in a vice, by the love of Christ. Very few of us know what it means to be held in a grip by the love of God; we are held by the constraint of our experience only. The one thing that held Paul, until there was nothing else on his horizon, was the love of God.[BP]

Reflection Questions

In what ways am I constrained by the love of Christ? What do I do or not do because of this constraint? What other call competes with the call to love?

GOD DOES NOT have to come and tell me what I must do for Him, He brings me into a relationship with Himself wherein I hear His call and understand what He wants me to do, and I do it out of sheer love to Him. To serve God is the deliberate love gift of a nature that has heard the call of God.[SSY]

GOD LOVES THE world so much that He goes all lengths to remove the wrong from it, and we must have the same kind of love. Any other kind of love for the world simply means that we take it as it is and are perfectly delighted with it. It is that sentiment which is the enemy of God.[BP]

Reflection Questions

Do I love the world sufficiently to spend and be spent so that God can manifest His grace through me until the wrong and the evil are removed?[BP]

O LORD, ENCHAIN me to Thyself with great bonds of adoring love; enwheel me around with Thy Providence for Thy purposes; enlarge me until I am more and more capable of being of use to Thee.[KGD]

FAITH IS BUILT on heroism. Consecration is the narrow, lonely way to over-flooding love. We are not called upon to live long on this planet, but we are called upon to be holy at any and every cost. If obedience costs you your life, then pay it.CD

Reflection Questions
Where do my ideas of love come from?
Do I consider popularity proof of love
or am I willing to be lonely to
experience God's love?

"LOVE IS OF GOD." It never came from the devil and never can go to the devil. When I am rightly related to God, the more I love the more blessing does He pour out on other lives. The reward of love is the capacity to pour out more love all the time, "hoping for nothing again." That is the essential nature of perfect love.GW

THE CHARGE IS made that because God gave Job back his material prosperity, therefore the whole argument of the Book falls to the ground; but the blessing of God on Job was nothing more than an outward manifestation accompanying the certainty he now possessed—that he loves God and that God loves him. It is the overflowing favour of God poured out on a loved son who has come through the ordeal and won his way straight through to God.CHI

Reflection Questions
What ordeal has God taken me through?
In what ways has obedience become easier
the more I have practiced it?

IN THE EARLY stages of our Christian experience we are inclined to hunt with delight for the commandments of our Lord in order to obey them out of our love for Him, but when that conscious obedience is assimilated and we begin to mature in our life with God, we obey His commandments unconsciously, until in the maturest stage of all we are simply children of God through whom God does His will, for the most part unconsciously to us.GW

IF JESUS CHRIST cannot alter me now, so that the alteration shows externally in my home life, in my business life, when is He going to alter me? What is going to transform me so that I can love my enemies, can pray for those that persecute me, if I cannot do it now? No suffering or discipline on my part will make me any different; the only thing that will make me different is being born again into the Kingdom of God. To look for death to make me holy is to make out that death, which is "the last enemy," is going to do what the Atonement cannot do.ᴳᵂ

Reflection Questions

Is the Spirit of God alive in me so that God has unlimited access to exercise His strength through me? What does God want me to build to further His kingdom?

WHETHER WE ARE Christians or not, we must all build; the point is that a Christian builds upon a different basis. If we build to please ourselves, we are building on the sand; if we build for the love of God, we are building on the rock.ᴼᴮᴴ

HAVE I THIS delight of intimacy, or am I trying to bend Almighty God to some end of my own? Am I asking Him to make me a particular type of saint? If through my love for Him I am discerning His voice, it is a proof that individuality has been effaced in the oneness of personal relationship. The real enemy to the delight of intimacy with Jesus is not sin, but individual relationships (cf. Luke 14:26). Distraction comes from intimacy with those who are not intimate with Jesus.[HGM]

Reflection Questions

What human relationships drain my strength and keep me from having an exclusive relationship with God?

SERVICE IS THE overflow of superabounding devotion, the echo of my identification with the nature of God. Service is the natural part of my life. God gets me into a relationship with Himself whereby I understand His call, then I do things out of sheer love for Him on my own account. To serve God is the deliberate love-gift of a nature that has heard the call of God.[CG]

I<small>T IS AN</small> easy business to say I love my enemies when I haven't any, but when I have an enemy, when a man has done me or those who belong to me, a desperate wrong, what is my attitude as a Christian to be? Does Jesus Christ mean that I have to ignore the rugged sense of justice which is in every man, and be a sentimentalist and say, "Oh yes, I forgive you"? What we are up against just now is the danger of not making the basis of forgiveness and peace the right kind. If it is not the basis of perfect justice, it will fail. We may succeed in calling a truce, but that is not peace, and before long we will be at it again.<small>HGM</small>

Reflection Questions

Do I consider myself strong because I am able to overlook sin? How is my understanding of peace wrong when I think it has nothing to do with justice?

O L<small>ORD</small>, <small>THIS</small> day lead me into some more of Thy gracious and wondrous doings. Put Thy loving hand of grace and power upon me this day.<small>KGD</small>

THERE IS NO such thing as God overlooking sin. That is where people make a great mistake with regard to God's love; they say "God is love and of course He will forgive sin": God is holy love and of course He cannot forgive sin. Therefore if God does forgive, there must be a reason that justifies Him in doing it. If I am forgiven without being altered by the forgiveness, forgiveness is a damage to me and a sign of unmitigated weakness on the part of God.^{HGM}

Reflection Questions

How has God's forgiveness altered me?

How does God's holiness strengthen me?

How does beauty energize me?

LORD, TOUCH WITH energizing power and sweet loving-kindness and beauty all our lives today; make it a time of the unveiling of Thy Face and power.^{KGD}

WHEN WE EXPERIENCE what we call being born again of the Spirit of God, we have "spurts" of faith, hope, love. They come, but we cannot grip them and they go. When we experience what we call sanctification those virtues abide; they are not accidental any more. The test of the life "hid with Christ in God" is not the experience of salvation or sanctification, but the relationship into which those experiences have led us. It is only by realizing the love of God in us by His grace that we are led by His entrancing power in us. ITWBP

Reflection Questions

Have my spurts of spiritual growth been transformed into spiritual strength? Have the seeds of faith and hope taken root in the soil of God's love? Am I growing in the strength of His grace?

BLESS US WITH waves of health and power. Show us more love that radiantly in Thy care we may go forth this day. Bless the strangers within our gates. KGD

IF WE CLING to things that are going to be shaken, then God will not prevent us being shaken with them, until we learn to let go of everything that He has condemned. We must be burned as fiercely pure as God is pure, and God will not leave us alone until we are. There is a difference between looking at God in the light of "love is God," and seeing Him in the light of "God is love." God is holy love, and nothing that is corruptible can come anywhere in His presence, it has to be burned and blazed right out of us.[NJ]

Reflection Questions

How can I expect to be made strong without first being made pure? How has God's kindness to me given me the strength to offer kindness to others?

WHEN WE HAVE wronged someone we love, the hard thing is not that he says something against us, but that he does not. That is the way our Lord judges, by His kindness (cf. Luke 15:21-24).[HGM]

CORRECTION IS NOT for the detection of faults, but in order to make perfect. We cannot be made good as dogs are, our wills must share in the making. God does not make us good in spite of ourselves. The terrors of God arise when God puts His finger on a man or a nation to draw them out of darkness into the light. Those who take God's way of coming into the light will find ultimately nothing but unspeakable joy and peace, life and love.NJ

Reflection Questions
How is God's love being perfected in me?
In what ways do joy, peace, and love characterize my life?

PERFECT LOVE IS to be expressed in actual life. Jesus is the love of God Incarnate. The only exhibition of the love of God in human flesh is our Lord, and John says "as He is, even so are we in this world." God expects His love to be manifested in our redeemed lives.CHI

Love with all your STRENGTH

IT IS EASY to say "God is love" when there is no war and when everything is going well; but it is not so easy to say when everything that happens actually gives the lie to it. For instance, when a man realizes he has an incurable disease, or a severe handicap in life, or when all that is dear has been taken from a man, for that man to say, as he faces these things, "God is love," means he has got hold of something the average man has missed.[LG]

Reflection Questions

What situation makes it difficult for me to say that God is love? What difficult situation has proven to me that God is love? What objections do I have to God's righteous standard of living?

GOD NEVER INSISTS on our obedience; human authority does. Our Lord does not give us rules and regulations; He makes very clear what the standard is, and if the relation of my spirit to Him is that of love, I will do all He wants me to do without the slightest hesitation. If I begin to object it is because I love someone else.[HGM]

GOD CREATED MAN to be His friend. If we are the friends of Jesus we have deliberately and carefully to lay down our life for Him. It is difficult, and thank God it is! When once the relationship of being the friends of Jesus is understood, we shall be called upon to exhibit to everyone we meet the love He has shown to us.ᴼᴮᴴ

Reflection Questions

In what ways does my friendship with Jesus make me a better friend? In what ways does the love of God make me a better lover of my family, friends, and even my enemies?

FRIENDSHIP WITH GOD is faith in action in relation to God and to our fellow-men. I love others as God has loved me, and I see in the ingratitude of others the ingratitude which I have exhibited to God.ᴺᴷᵂ

Love with all your STRENGTH

THE ONLY WAY in which the Kingdom of God can be established is by the love of God as revealed in the Cross of Jesus Christ, not by the lovingkindness of a backboneless being without justice or righteousness or truth. The background of God's love is holiness. His is not a compromising love, and the Kingdom of our Lord can only be brought in by means of His love at work in regeneration. Then when we are regenerated we must not insult God by imagining that in dealing with our fellow-men we can afford to ignore the need for Redemption and simply be kind and gentle and loving to all.[PR]

Reflection Questions
Do I insult God by ignoring the need for Redemption? What sin or sinners do I think are stronger than the power of God's redeeming grace?

NOTHING IS TOO hard for God, no sin too difficult for His love to overcome, not a failure but He can make it a success.[LG]

IF JESUS HAD been loyal to His earthly mother, He would have been a traitor to His Father's purpose. Obedience to the call of Christ nearly always costs everything to two people—the one who is called, and the one who loves that one. We put sensitive loyalty to relationships in place of loyalty to Jesus; every other love is put first, and He has to take the last place. We will readily give up sin and worldliness, but God calls us to give up the very closest, noblest and most right tie we have, if it enters into competition with His call. Beware of the inclination to dictate to God as to what you will allow to happen if you obey Him.ssy

Reflection Questions
In what ways does my loyalty to
Jesus take second place?

CHRISTIANITY IS NOT a thing of times and seasons, but of God and faith. Drink deep and full of the love of God and you will not demand the impossible from earth's loves, and the love of wife and child, of husband and friend, will grow holier and healthier and simpler and grander.LG

Love with all your STRENGTH

IF WE LOOK for God in the physical domain we shall see Him nowhere; if we look for Him in the kingdom on the inside, in the moral relationships, we shall find Him all the time. We lose faith in God when we are hurt in the physical domain and God does not do what we want; we forget that He is teaching us to rely on His love. Watch some people and you will wonder how a human being can support such anguish; yet instead of being full of misery, they are the opposite; they seem to be held by a power that baffles all human intelligence, to have a spiritual energy we know nothing of. The waters are real, and the fire is real, but Paul claims that the relationship to God holds.SHL

Reflection Questions

In what ways has God's love supported me through times of tears and human tragedy?

GOD IS LOVE—a puzzle text, to be solved slowly, as with tears and penitence, by prayer and joy, by vision and faith, and, last, by death.LG

WHEN ONCE WE realize that we cannot love our enemies, we cannot bless them that curse us, we cannot come anywhere near the standard revealed in the Sermon on the Mount, then we are in a condition to receive from God the disposition that will enable us to love our enemies, to pray for those that despitefully use us, to do good to those that hate us.SSM

Reflection Questions

What fires of refinement are at work in my life? Do I resist the searing heat or do I submit to the purifying flames of persecution and adversity, knowing that through them I will be made strong?

WHENEVER THERE IS a tendency to turn aside, we will find God is a consuming fire: He will hold and hurt cruelly, and we may cry out to Him to let us go, but He will not let us go. God loves us too much to let us go, and He will burn and burn until there is nothing left but the purity that is as pure as He is—unless we determine to side with the impure and become as reprobate silver.OBH

SPIRITUALLY, MORALLY, AND physically the saint is brought clean through, triumphant, out of the wreck wrought by tribulation, anguish, persecution, famine, nakedness, peril and sword. Whatever may be the experiences of life, whether terrible and devastating or monotonous, it makes no difference, they are all rendered impotent, because they cannot separate us from the love of God, which is in Christ Jesus Our Lord.SHL

Reflection Questions

What forces are at work to separate me from God's love? What circumstance or relationship is luring me away from God and leaving me weak and ineffective?

WHETHER WE ARE Christians or not, we must all build; the point is that a Christian builds upon a different basis. If we build to please ourselves, we are building on the sand; if we build for the love of God, we are building on the rock.OBH

IF THE LOVE of God were presented as having no hatred of wrong and of sin and the devil, it would simply mean that God's love is not so strong as our love. The stronger and higher and more emphatic the love, the more intense is its obverse, hate. God loves the world so much that He hates with a perfect hatred the thing that is twisting men away from Him.[BP]

Reflection Questions

In what areas have I stepped outside the safe boundaries of God's love because I do not yet hate the things that God hates— the things that lure people away from God?

NATURALLY WE ALWAYS want to go somewhere else, but the love of God works just where we are, and His love works irrespective of persons.[OBH]

WE MUST BEWARE of letting natural affinities hinder our walking in love. One of the most cruel ways of killing love is by disdain built on natural affinities. To be guided by our affinities is a natural tendency, but spiritually this tendency must be denied, and as we deny it we find that God gives us affinity with those for whom we have no natural affinity.OBH

Reflection Questions
What good thing do I find difficult to do?
How would it be easier if I allowed the power
of God's love to do it through me?

GOD'S COMMANDS ARE made to the life of His Son in us, not to our human nature; consequently all that God tells us to do is always humanly difficult; but it becomes divinely easy immediately we obey because our obedience has behind it all the omnipotent power of the grace of God.OBH

THE DIFFERENCE BETWEEN lust and love comes just here. Lust is—I must have it at once. Love can wait. Lust makes me impulsively impatient, I want to take short cuts, and do things right off. Love can wait endlessly. If I have ever seen God and been touched by Him and the Spirit of God has entered into me, I am willing to wait for Him; I wait in the certainty that He will come.[PH]

Reflection Questions

What good thing is God asking me to wait to receive? How does waiting strengthen my faith, increase my love, and intensify my desire for holiness?

THE LOVE OF God and His forgiveness are the first things we experience, we are not prepared as yet to recognize His other attributes of holiness and justice because that will mean death to everything that does not partake of God's nature.[OPG]

Love with all your STRENGTH

WHEN PAUL SAID, "For me to live is Christ," he did not mean that he did not live for anything else; but that the dominant note, the great consuming passion underneath everything, was his love for Jesus Christ—it explained everything he did.[PH]

Reflection Questions

In what ways is Christ my consuming passion? How does my love for Him dominate every thing that I do? How does my devotion to Him keep me radiant even in the darkest circumstances?

UNDAUNTED RADIANCE IS not built on anything passing, but on the love of God that nothing can alter. The experiences of life, terrible or monotonous, are impotent to touch "the love of God, which is in Christ Jesus our Lord."[RTR]

GOD IS THE King of my heart, King of my soul, King of my mind, King of my strength; nothing other than God; and the working out of it is that we show the same love to our fellow-men as God has shown us. That is the external aspect of this internal relationship, the sovereign preference of my person for God. The love of the heart for Jesus, the life laid down for Jesus, the mind thinking only for Jesus, the strength given over to Jesus, the will working only the will of God, and the ear of the personality hearing only what God has to say.ITWBP

Reflection Questions

What aspect of my life—heart, soul, mind, strength—am I reserving for myself? What fear keeps me from allowing God's love to penetrate every aspect of my being?

IT DOES NOT matter where a man may get to in the way of tribulation or anguish, none of it can wedge in between and separate him from the love of God in Christ Jesus.RTR

Love with all your STRENGTH

GET INTO THE habit of recalling what Jesus was like when He was here. Picture what He did and what He said, recall His gentleness and tenderness as well as His strength and sternness. Then say, "That is what God is like." I do not think it would be difficult for us to love Jesus if He went in and out among us as in the days of His flesh, healing the sick and diseased, restoring the distracted, putting right those who were wrong, reclaiming backsliders—I do not think it would be difficult for us to love Him.CHI

Reflection Questions

What false picture do I have of Jesus?
How is that keeping me from loving Him
fully and loving others on His behalf?

IF JESUS CHRIST has lifted us in love and grace, we must show that love to someone else. God will surround us with ample opportunity of doing to others as He has done to us.SSY

THE CROSS IS the supreme moment in Time and Eternity, and it is the concentrated essence of the very nature of the Divine love. God lays down His life in the very creation we utilize for our own selfish ends. God lays down His life in His long-suffering patience with the civilized worlds which men have erected on God's earth in defiance of all He has revealed. The Self-expenditure of God for His enemies in the life and death of our Lord Jesus Christ, becomes the great bridge over the gulf of sin whereby human love may cross over and be embraced by the Divine love, the love that never fails.^{TPH}

Reflection Questions

What was the supreme moment in my life when I crossed the bridge from sinful, self-love to the Divine embrace of God's love? In what ways has that love changed my attitudes and actions toward other people?

THANK GOD THAT we have the glorious fighting chance of identifying ourselves with our Lord's interests in other people in the love that never fails.^{TPH}

Index of Selections

Note to the Reader

The publisher invites you to share your response to the message of this book by writing Discovery House Publishers, P.O. Box 3566, Grand Rapids, MI 49501, U.S.A. or by calling 1-800-653-8333. For information about other Discovery House publications, contact us at the same address and phone number.